The future of churches

The UK has over 39,000 church buildings. The restrictions of COVID-19, resulting in reduced funding and fewer worshippers, has clouded the future for many of them.

Yet churches remain a vital and much loved part of the UK's history and heritage and we can't let them fall into neglect and disuse. There is hope. More and more churches are adapting to the modern world and the needs of their communities, providing not just spiritual comforts but a range of valuable services to local people such as foodbanks and youth clubs.

We must build on this, and encourage people of all sorts and from all backgrounds to find hope and relevance in their local churches.

If you care as much as I do about the future of these much loved buildings, do get involved with the National Churches Trust debate about churches and help shape their future.

nationalchurchestrust.org/futureofchurches – #futureofchurches

Sir Michael Palin, Vice President, National Churches Trust

The National Churches Trust is the only UK wide charity supporting church buildings open for worship. We are unique in being able to help churches of all denominations, both those that are listed and those that are unlisted.

Our vision is that church buildings across the UK are well maintained, open to everyone, sustainable and valued. So we have asked 17 people, including heritage experts, leaders of charities that use church buildings for community purposes, clergy and a poet to share with us their vision for their future.

We want to start a national debate. At the heart of this are some simple questions:

- Why do church buildings matter?
- How can we as a society preserve their magnificent heritage?
- How can more church buildings be made into community hubs?
- What is the best way to pay for the upkeep of church buildings?

Right now, many church buildings are in danger as they do not have the money to fund urgent repairs and maintenance or to put in essential facilities such a toilets and kitchens. In fact over 900 churches are on the Historic England 'Heritage at Risk Register', with many more in a parlous state in Scotland, Wales and Northern Ireland.

Our nation's church buildings are a unique asset. It would be a tremendous mistake to squander this much loved inheritance which we calculate provides at least £50 billion in economic and social value to the UK each year.

I invite you to read this collection of essays and then tell us what you think. At the back of this publication there is a consultation form, and this can also be filled in online at **nationalchurchestrust.org/futureofchurches**

At the National Churches Trust we will do everything we can to support church buildings in need. We all stand to lose if we let them disappear.

Luke March, Chairman, National Churches Trust

Published by The National Churches Trust 2021
Copyright © National Churches Trust
ISBN 978-1-3999-1244-0

Contents

Churches are vital to levelling up

I'd like to express my thanks to all the contributors to The Future of the UK's Church Buildings. They all recognise the importance of churches, chapels and meeting houses to the UK and the value they bring to our society.

In 2020, the National Churches Trust published The House of Good, which for the first time quantified the economic and social value of church buildings to the UK.

Since then, HM Treasury has changed the way it measures the benefits of wellbeing to individuals and to society in its Green Book. This means that we can now say that church buildings contribute over £50 billion in economic and social value each year to the UK. They play a vital role in social cohesion, helping the disadvantaged and in levelling up.

By way of introduction, in the first essay of The Future of the UK's Church Buildings, I write about the findings of The House of Good and the importance of church buildings.

Claire Walker
Chief Executive, National Churches Trust

6

HERITAGE

Harry Mount
The last chance saloon

10

Andrew Stokes
Open the doors to tourism and churches

14

PLACES OF WORSHIP

Salford Cathedral
© Diocese of Salford

The Right Reverend John Arnold
The future of our churches

26

COMMUNITY

Barbara Eifler
Inspired to make music

42

Simon Thomson
Helping to fight hunger

46

THE UNITED KINGDOM

Christopher Catling
Wales – Go thy way

62

Stuart Beattie
Scotland's churches

66

NATIONAL CHURCHES TRUST

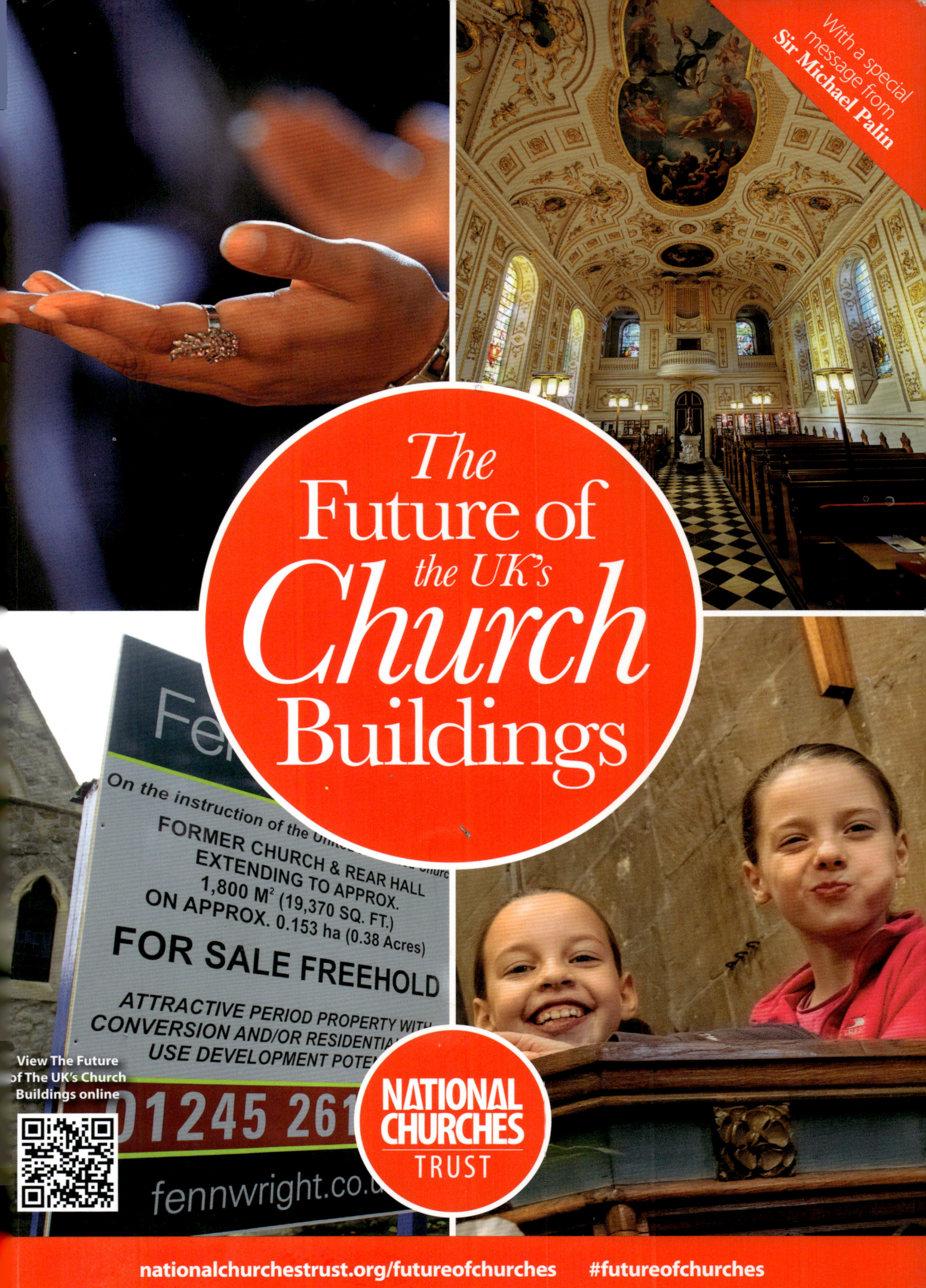

St Mary's church, Horncastle, Lincolnshire © ExploreChurches

Jay Hulme
In the footsteps of your ancestors
18

St Nicholas' Church, Leicester
© Jay Hulme

Peter Ainsworth
The biggest single heritage challenge
22

Rev Lucy Winkett
Society needs church buildings
30

Rev Eve Pitts and Anthony Pitts
Bringing people together
34

Rev Canon John McGinley
The great good place
38

Dominic Grieve
The communal benefits of sacred space
50

Rt Hon Stephen Timms MP
Churches in the pandemic
54

Alexander Stafford MP
Churches do still matter, as they always have done
58

Dr Julian Litten FRA
England's rural churches through all ages
70

A farmer's market at St Giles, Shipbourne

Iain Greenway
An iconic part of the historic environment of Northern Ireland
74

THE FUTURE OF THE UK's CHURCH BUILDINGS

Churches are vital to levelling up

Claire Walker
Chief Executive, National Churches Trust

"Church buildings help to level up every single day; it is what they do and have always done, and The House of Good study makes clear just how valuable this is to British society."

In October 2020, the National Churches Trust published The House of Good. This report quantified, for the first time ever, the social value of all church buildings in the UK. Not just the bricks and mortar but the welfare and wellbeing they create in our communities.

In 2020, our researchers estimated that the total social value of UK church buildings is around £12.4 billion a year. That's about what the NHS spent on mental health in 2018.

The statistics in The House of Good are underpinned by figures established by HM Treasury to evaluate policies and put a financial value on things that cannot be bought and sold. For example the benefits derived from a foodbank run by volunteers or the satisfaction that comes from a moment of quiet reflection at the back of a church.

The methods used by the Treasury to assess policies and determine their values are published in The Green Book. This is the nationally recognised standard for measuring such hard to quantify values and these methods have now been revised. They enable us to say that the economic and social value of church buildings is much higher than we thought.

One change to The Green Book adjusts the way the Treasury supports policy interventions and prioritises those that are intended to address regional economic disparities. It is intended to enable ministers and other decision makers to fully understand what investments they need to make to most effectively drive the delivery of the levelling up agenda. The other change determines how wellbeing is valued.

The prioritisation of policy interventions that support the government's levelling up agenda effectively confirms what The House of Good made crystal clear in 2020, namely that church buildings provide massive social support for people and communities throughout the UK. Furthermore, many of the most socially active churches are in deprived areas. They make a particularly important contribution towards achieving greater equality.

Measuring the value of wellbeing

Provision of services ranging from drug and alcohol counselling to youth groups offers benefits to the volunteers who run them as well as to those who use them. They bring people together for the common good and strengthen communities. In short, church buildings help to level up every single day: it's what they do and always have done.

Besides prioritising efforts to create a more equitable society, The Green Book has changed the way the government measures wellbeing. This new guidance was published in July 2021.

The House of Good used the WELLBY to put a price on the non-market value of the activities taking place in church buildings. This is a new tool and its name is short for Wellbeing Guidance for Appraisal. In 2020, our report used a very conservative rate to reach the total of £12.4 billion a year for the social value of church buildings in the UK.

In July 2021, HM Treasury adopted the WELLBY as its primary measure for wellbeing. But, it officially recommended that a unit of wellbeing, a WELLBY, be given an average monetary value of £13,000. This is more than **five times higher** than the average figure used in The House of Good.

>>

"Last year the National Churches Trust awarded grants of over £1.7 million to help support church buildings."

Churches are vital to levelling up

\>\>

In short, by using HM Treasury's figures, we find that the yearly social value of churches in the UK and the activities that take place in them is about £55.7 billion. That is twice as much as local authorities spend on adult social care.

For every £1 invested in a church, the return is over £16. That's four or five times more than would be expected in other spheres of investment.

Churches are vital to their communities

Last year, the National Churches Trust awarded grants of over £1.7 million to help support church buildings. In 2021, thanks to the support of the Heritage Stimulus Fund, we have been able to provide even more.

We contribute to the cost of repairs to the fabric of church buildings and we also help make them fit for the 21st century by supporting the installation of kitchens and toilets. We know how vital churches are to their communities and we want to help them continue to be so.

We cannot do this alone. Investment from philanthropic trusts, individuals and from central and local government is essential to keep churches open and in good repair with up to date community facilities.

Support for church buildings is a vital step towards addressing the inequalities that have developed in the UK and are holding back the lives of millions of our fellow citizens.

Claire Walker

Claire Walker has been the Chief Executive of the National Churches Trust since 2011. She works closely with Trustees to provide strategic leadership for the charity which is the leading voice for church buildings in the UK.

www.nationalchurchestrust.org

Top: Churches bring people together who are willing to help others © Diocese of Westminster

WHAT WE FOUND

WHAT WE THOUGHT
The 2020 research showed that the total economic and social value of church buildings to the UK was **£12.4bn**.

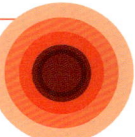

WHAT WE KNOW NOW
Today, HM Treasury Green Book calculations show the true value to be **£55bn**, more than four times higher than previously thought.

TOTAL VALUE

£55 billion per year

THE FUTURE OF THE UK's CHURCH BUILDINGS

HERITAGE

The last chance Saloon

Harry Mount
Author and journalist and Editor of The Oldie.

"How do you retain the ancientness and the reverence, and make the buildings useful at the same time?"

A friend of mine, who works in the Foreign Office, once told me how she was longing for her next post in France after a spell in America. She had missed what she called 'les vieilles pierres' – the old stones.

When lockdown ended, I was hungry for old stones and, in particular, for churches.

Stuck in London for the pandemic, I'd been deprived of them for an agonisingly long time.

The first I went to was St Mary's, Warren, Pembrokeshire – a 14th-century church with an enchanting, late-medieval spire you can see from miles in every direction.

I felt a Ready-Brek glow just gazing at the old stones of the church from the outside, with nothing beyond it except empty fields, the Castlemartin military range and the sea beyond.

Inside, the glow intensified at that good old feeling you get on entering a church: of silence and a slightly musty hit of ancient dust and new furniture polish, mixed with reverence.

Larkin's "Church Going"

It's impossible to talk about these things without thinking about Philip Larkin's "Church Going". The poem was published in 1955 but, even then, he was asking the question the Church of England is asking that much more desperately today:

...wondering too
When churches fall completely out of use
What we shall turn them into, if we shall keep
A few cathedrals chronically on show,
Their parchment, plate, and pyx in locked cases,
And let the rest rent-free to rain and sheep.
Shall we avoid them as unlucky places?

Larkin ended that great poem on a semi-optimistic note:

Someone will forever be surprising
A hunger in himself to be more serious,
And gravitating with it to this ground,
Which, he once heard, was proper to grow wise in,
If only that so many dead lie round.

I'm sure he's right. We won't see the bulldozers move in on St Mary's, Warren, or any other ancient church – partly because of that respect for the dead and the feeling of seriousness Larkin refers to; partly because of planning rules.

What will happen to the buildings?

But what will happen to the buildings? Several other Pembrokeshire churches near St Mary's have already closed in recent years. Their structure is kept in good nick. They remain consecrated for the odd service.

But it's hard to see them opening up for regular services with big congregations ever again. What to do with the churches?

The Archbishop of Canterbury and the higher echelons of the Church of England did not cover themselves with glory during the pandemic.

They rushed to close the church doors just when calm, beautiful, ancient places were most required; just when huge, empty buildings were the safest place for a few congregants – even more so for the lone church visitor like I was at St Mary's, Warren.

Please, God, we won't face such bleak days again. And, if and when the pandemic disappears, or remains at a low, manageable level, those two qualities of most of our churches – old stones and a quiet place of strong, religious feeling – will remain vanishingly rare, particularly in our city centres, ravaged by modern development.

Those qualities are even more powerful in the digital age, when so many of us – including me – spend so much of our days staring at an unlovely, modern, glass screen.

>>

THE FUTURE OF THE UK's CHURCH BUILDINGS

"New uses needn't come at the sacrifice of the church's original, crucial, spiritual purpose."

The last chance Saloon

>>

Squaring the circle

But how do you square the circle? How do you retain the ancientness and the reverence, and make the buildings useful at the same time?

I'm afraid there has to be a compromise. The writer Simon Jenkins has put it well in the past. Empty churches – unless they are unusually well-endowed – will have to bite the bullet and lend part of their fabric to commercial purposes.

Plenty of them do this already, of course – renting out the church or the church hall for everything from business AGMs to pop concerts.

That's easy enough in a city; more difficult in rural Britain. I'm afraid that the more remote a building, the greater the compromise will inevitably be.

In extremis – and only if necessary to pay for the upkeep of a church – the church nave could be converted to residential use, with the choir (if there is one) and chancel still fenced off for religious observance, with access guaranteed to worshippers. Any conversion work must be reversible in the unlikely event of a return to growing congregations.

If the rural migration from cities that happened during lockdown is maintained, church space will be even more valuable – as remote offices and cafés.

These new uses needn't come at the sacrifice of the church's original, crucial, spiritual purpose. I have often sat in the café at St Mary Aldermary, Christopher Wren's marvellous Gothic church in the City of London – and have felt a deeply spiritual feeling.

The ability to sit and stare

Many times, I've found it easier to pray, staring at Wren's sublime fan vaults, double macchiato in hand, than I have when kneeling in prayer elsewhere. The ability to sit and stare while sitting at a café table, doing not very much, produces the right sort of mood for thoughtful contemplation.

Of course, lots of uses must be forbidden: betting shops and sex shops spring to mind as unacceptable. But I see no reason why bars shouldn't be allowed in the unconsecrated parts of churches – and I stress that this is only in those churches that are facing closure or bankruptcy if they don't embrace commercial alternatives.

So many churches are in the last chance saloon – better that they should become holy altars with saloons attached than disappear for ever.

Harry Mount

Henry Mount is an author and journalist who is editor of The Oldie and a frequent contributor to the Daily Mail and the Daily Telegraph. His books include Amo, Amas, Amat… And All That, How England Made the English – from Hedgerows to Heathrow and Harry's Mount's Odyssey: Ancient Greece in the Footsteps of Odysseus.

NATIONAL CHURCHES TRUST

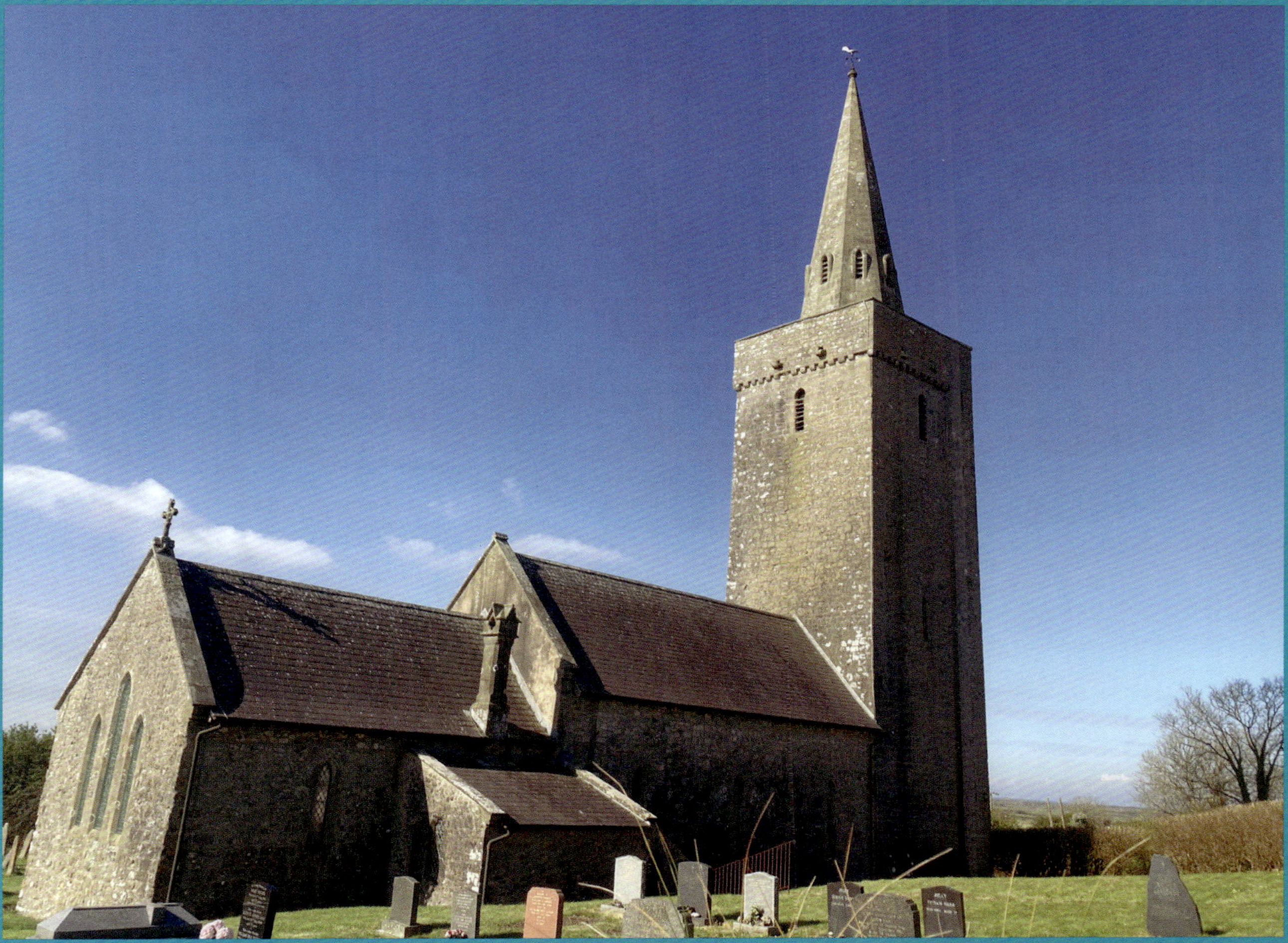

Above: Philip Larkin
© Album / Alamy Stock Photo
Left: The cafe at St Mary Aldermary, London © Harry Mount
Top: St Mary's, Warren, Pembrokeshire © Harry Mount

HERITAGE

Open the doors:
Tourism *and* churches

Andrew Stokes
Director, VisitEngland

> *"Visiting churches puts people in touch with local history like nowhere else."*

Our statistics and research demonstrate the importance of churches and places of worship to our tourism offer.

Looking back at VisitEngland's 2019 annual survey of visitor attractions in England, visitor numbers, both domestic and international, to places of worship were up 7% compared to 2018 with revenue generated up 6%. St Paul's Cathedral, Westminster Abbey and Canterbury Cathedral were all in the top 20 most 'paid for' visitor attractions in England, ranking fourth, seventh and eleventh respectively. And when looking longer-term, visits to places of worship in England have increased 5% on average each year during the three years from 2017 to 2019.

Statistics from VisitBritain show that our history and heritage are highly regarded attributes for overseas visitors. More than a fifth, 21%, of all inbound trips include a visit to a religious building in the UK, equating to about seven million visits annually. Overseas travellers that visit a religious building as part of their trip usually spend £7 billion in the UK overall every year.

Visiting churches and places of worship are also a draw for travellers interested in finding out about their ancestors and with the UK's strong links to countries in the Commonwealth, families from around the world pay their respects at war graves and in cemeteries to see the final resting place of loved ones.

Beauty, history and sheer wonder

The outstanding variety, beauty, history and sheer wonder of England's churches and places of worship are also very important in boosting visits right across our regions, including to destinations not always on the tourism radar.

Nestled both across the countryside and within our towns and cities, they encourage visitors to explore a destination year-round and have an important role in extending the tourism season, drawing visitors across the shoulder and low seasons. They also provide people with a moment away from the hustle and bustle of life not only to reflect but also to learn more about an area's wider history and culture, telling the story of a destination and giving a sense of place and community, and often encouraging visits to other businesses and attractions, supporting local economies.

Visiting churches puts people in touch with local history like nowhere else – getting them to think about the residents behind the buildings, statues and plaques that commemorate local life, creating lasting connections that inspire future travel.

Supporting churches

The National Churches Trust has also been showing a new way forward for churches to benefit directly from tourism spend. The 'Experiences by ExploreChurches' project, which VisitEngland supported through the Discover England Fund, brings churches to life for today's visitors. By working with other organisations in their area, this project has supported churches in creating exciting itineraries that bring extra added value to a day-out and the wider visitor experience.

It is also timely to reflect on the impact on the tourism industry from the COVID-19 pandemic and the challenges ahead including for attractions. VisitEngland's latest annual attractions survey, for 2020, underscores the severe impact on visitor attractions from the COVID-19 pandemic with a 65% drop in visitors overall compared to 2019 and a 55% decline in revenue. These declines were driven by site closures associated with lockdowns and opening restrictions and the significant contraction of inbound and domestic tourism. The fall in visitor numbers last year to England's attractions was most marked for museums and galleries, other historic properties and places of worship, many of which rely on overseas visitors.

>>

> "63% of those surveyed said they anticipate taking a day-trip at some stage."

Open the doors:
Tourism and churches

While we can see the green shoots of recovery, businesses have lost many months of vital trading. We are forecasting domestic tourism spending in Britain this year to be well below 2019 levels, £51.4 billion in 2021, just more than half of the £91.6 billion in 2019. Looking at inbound tourism, our forecast is for £5.3 billion in overseas visitor spending in the UK this year, less than a quarter of the £28.4 billion in 2019, with our cities and city visitor attractions particularly hard hit.

Church on the must see list

Extending the season through the lean shoulder months and continuing to build confidence in taking domestic overnight and day-trips is crucial.

At the time of writing our latest consumer sentiment research, published on 17 September, shows that domestic travel intentions are up from the same time last year and most people still plan to continue with their UK trip even if all overseas travel restrictions lift. Looking at day-trips, 70% of those surveyed, representing 38.3 million UK adults, anticipated taking one this autumn or later. And with many churches being on the must see list for day-trippers now is the time to encourage visitors in.

Businesses and attractions including churches and places of worship have been working flat-out to welcome customers back safely, adapting and innovating to meet new ways of working and still providing a great visitor experience. Our We're Good To Go industry standard is well established with more than 565 churches and cathedrals in England registered on the scheme, ready to safely welcome back visitors.

So we hope people will consider revisiting or exploring somewhere new and having an extra day out. We know our tourism businesses and visitor attractions will be very pleased to welcome visitors back.

Andrew Stokes

Andrew Stokes joined VisitEngland in 2016 as the England Director. Prior to this he spent 16 years as CEO of Marketing Manchester. He worked on the 2002 Commonwealth Games and the creation of a major events strategy for the city region.

www.visitengland.com

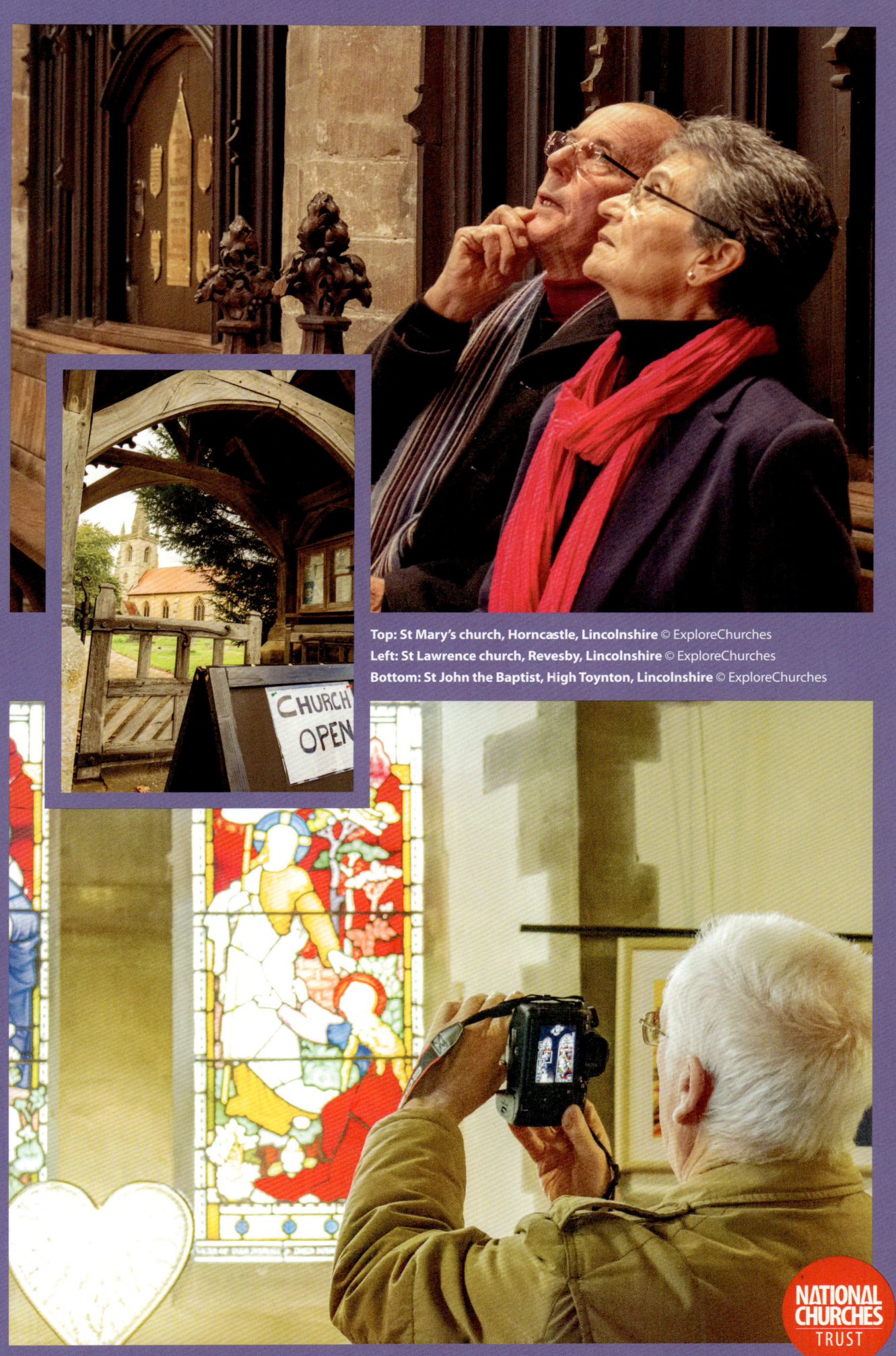

Top: St Mary's church, Horncastle, Lincolnshire © ExploreChurches
Left: St Lawrence church, Revesby, Lincolnshire © ExploreChurches
Bottom: St John the Baptist, High Toynton, Lincolnshire © ExploreChurches

HERITAGE

In the footsteps of your ancestors

Jay Hulme
Poet

"When you walk into an ancient church you walk in the footsteps of your ancestors."

I attend St Nicholas' Church, Leicester. St Nicholas' was built in 879, is radically inclusive, and filled with members of the LGBT+ community. People who attend services here range from almost ninety years old, down through middle age, through people in their twenties, like me, right down to a toddler, whose birth announcement still sits clipped to the priest's lectern – the message from his mothers an outpouring of love and gratitude for this found community.

People often say communities like the one at St Nick's can be created anywhere - and that is true, but the ancient building is important. Especially to young people. Especially now. To explain why old buildings matter, even (and especially) to the young people that are often cited as the reason for their closure, we must look at the world from the perspective of a 'young person'.

When I was a child we didn't have a computer. I remember the excitement of the internet being installed. I remember being barred from using it because we had dial up and were expecting a phone call. I remember my Dad's first Nokia phone. I remember getting a 'big telly' – all cathode ray tubes and at least two foot deep at the back. I remember watching a VHS tape until it broke. Getting cassette tapes from my Grandparents for my birthday.

I remember getting a DVD player. A CD player. The record collection getting shuffled off into storage. I remember being allowed out to play on busy roads. And then not being allowed.

I remember phones pouring into schools. And being banned from schools. I have lived through multiple worldwide financial crashes, eleven UK Governments, and a worldwide pandemic. I am only 24 years old. Everything is changing at a terrifyingly rapid speed. Things that were sci-fi only ten years ago are now utterly mundane. For people younger than me, this change seems even faster, even more unsettling.

With the rise of short-term tenancies, the 'gig' economy, and most goods being made to last a few years at most, we do not have much to hold on to. Everything changes. We stumble through a world where constancy and security are unthinkable. Statistically, people in their early twenties stay in tenancies for less than a year. I have a friend who has lived in eight places in six years. This is not unusual, and almost never by choice.

For young people today there is no continuity. Nothing stays the same.

Wider human experience

Ancient buildings give us that sense of continuity, a sense of being part of something bigger, and a connection with all that has come before. Ancient churches, in particular, give us this in ways no other ancient buildings do. Not only are churches often the oldest buildings in any given place, they are also the oldest buildings that have been continually used for a specific purpose. They are constant in a way nothing else is anymore.

When you walk into an ancient church you walk in the footsteps of your ancestors, both in the literal, genetic, sense of the word, and in the broader sense, encompassing all of those who have come before. You are rooted to the wider human experience.

>>

"Ancient churches, in particular, give us this in ways no other ancient buildings do."

THE FUTURE OF THE UK's CHURCH BUILDINGS

> "In old church buildings we are reminded of our place in the vastness of human experience."

In the footsteps of your ancestors

>>

When the service begins, you know that what is happening has happened in this place for hundreds of years – the form changing and evolving through time, but still, somehow, the same – with a constancy of feeling, and intent.

When Covid ravaged Leicester, when ambulances rushed along the main road outside the church one after the other, sirens screaming like harbingers of the death that was all around us, the church was, to me, and to other members of the community, an important reminder.

Even as we couldn't celebrate that Christmas in church, we considered the 1141 Christmases that this building had seen. The multiple pandemics it had stood through. The death and devastation and change it had witnessed. And when we opened the church doors again, we continued – the service changing, slightly, to accommodate restrictions – but still, somehow, the same.

In old church buildings we are reminded of our place in the vastness of human experience. We are reminded that life has stretched on long before us, and will continue long after we are gone. We are given unparalleled perspective, in a world that is so often short-sighted

Old churches are tapestries, records of the past. Of love and loss, birth and death, of poverty, and plague, and dizzying success. The stone tells stories people never can. The buildings change and evolve, and somehow remain the same. The services continue.

We sing and weep and everything in between, stood in these buildings that have held the lives of hundreds of thousands of people. Ancient churches stand, steadfast and ever constant, amidst the rushing flow of time. It is a privilege to shelter in them, even for a short while.

St Nicholas' Church has seen almost 60,000 Sundays. Hopefully we can continue to treasure and protect her, so that she, and many other ancient churches, may stand to see almost 60,000 more.

Jay Hulme

Jay Hulme is an award winning transgender performance poet, speaker and educator. Alongside his writing and regular performances he teaches in schools, performs sensitivity reads, and consults and speaks at events and conferences on the importance of diversity in the media, and more specifically transgender inclusion and rights.

www.jayhulme.com

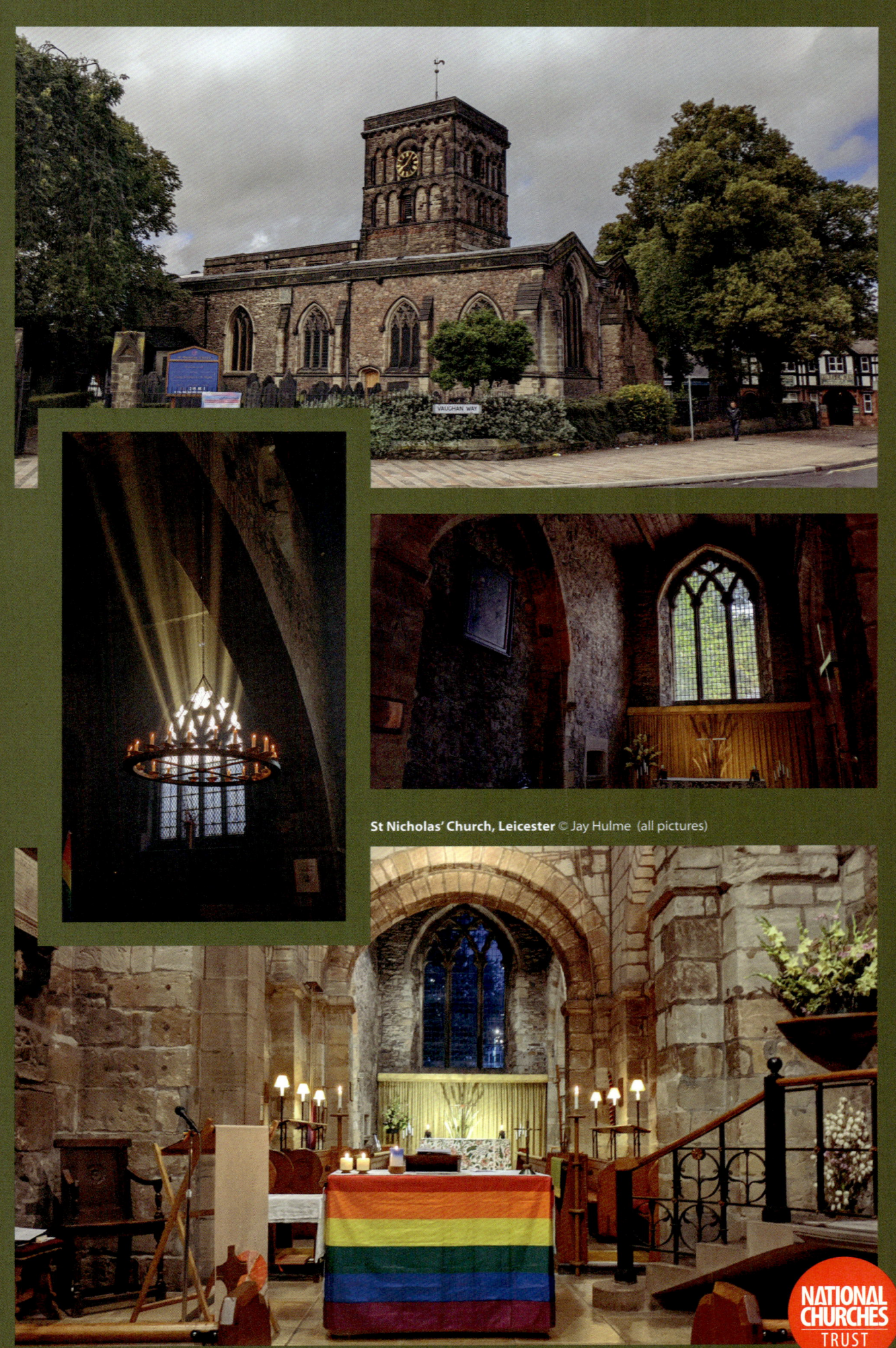

St Nicholas' Church, Leicester © Jay Hulme (all pictures)

HERITAGE

The biggest *single heritage* challenge

The late Peter Ainsworth
Chairman of The Churches Conservation Trust 2016-2021

"The Church of England is responsible for 45% of all Grade I listed buildings in England."

We are a national charity – with a national collection of buildings of international importance. But each one of those churches is unique and individual and individually loved, supported and cared for – by you and thousands like you.

I don't pretend that the task we share is easy, or getting easier.

We now have 356 churches in our care. The number creeps up every year. Of course on one level they belong to the CCT; they have been vested in the CCT. So we have a responsibility to make sure that they are looked after.

But – just as importantly – they belong to where they are. To where you are. That is why our Strategic Plan involves a much closer engagement with local communities. The CCT's task is to help local groups to look after what matters to them. To you. For now and forever.

Inspired by faith and certainty

"Placemaking" has become a fashionable buzz-word. Each one of these churches has a powerful spirit of place; the place it occupies. The spirit is invisibly connected to those who laboured to build, craft, and make these places; and who are buried nearby. They were inspired by faith and certainty. Those are not fashionable buzz words today.

And that is a problem. It's not a new one. In his great poem "Dover Beach" Matthew Arnold wrote that:

The Sea of Faith
Was once, too, at the full,
And round Earth's shore
Lay like the folds of a bright girdle furled;
But now I only hear
Its melancholy, long, withdrawing roar
Retreating, to the breath
Of the night wind, down vast edges drear
And naked shingles of the world.

That was in 1867.

In May 1954 the Archbishop of Canterbury launched "Save Our Churches Week". He said that the decline in congregations meant that "over 2,000 churches must be helped at once to be saved from decay and ruin".

And now, in 2020, there are some 12,000 listed churches in England. The vast majority are in rural areas with small populations and a rapidly declining number of active Christian worshipers. Did you know that the Church of England is responsible for 45% of all Grade I listed buildings in England?

Protecting our national heritage

The Parish system, for centuries the mainstay of religious, cultural and social life, simply cannot cope – although there are a few exceptions – with the burden of its built inheritance. That system hasn't coped for a few generations now and it is unlikely to do so in future. I wonder how many current church wardens are under sixty years old.

>>

"Our historic churches are an emblem of what and who we are in our own eyes, in our own communities and in the eyes of the world."

THE FUTURE OF THE UK's CHURCH BUILDINGS

> "We cannot convert people back to Christian faith. That's not our job. But we can demonstrate the connection which exists between a sense of history and access to beautiful places."

The biggest single heritage challenge

>>

What happens next to the historic parish church is probably the biggest single question facing anyone charged with a duty to protect our national heritage. It's not just a problem for the Church of England or the Government. Our historic churches are an emblem of what and who we are in our own eyes, in our own communities and in the eyes of the world. So what is to be done?

The story of our country

We are keen to demonstrate that we have the people, the skills, the knowledge, the access to the crafts which will be needed to help sustain our historic places of worship. We know all about rotten roofs and gutters and damp and woodworm. We have been tackling this stuff for over 50 years. We believe that we have ideas and techniques and commercial contacts which can help.

We cannot convert people back to Christian faith. That's not our job. But we can demonstrate the connection which exists between a sense of history and access to beautiful places and thoughtful happiness and a sense of wellbeing and a pride in where we live. Our churches tell the story of our country, ourselves, in every place where they stand – or fall.

Extract from a speech given in 2020.

Peter Ainsworth

Peter Ainsworth was appointed Chairman of The Churches Conservation Trust in July 2016 and served in this position until his death in April 2021. His involvement in heritage dates back to 1995, when he was appointed Parliamentary Private Secretary to the Secretary of State for National Heritage. He was a member of the DCMS Select Committee in 2009-10.

www.visitchurches.org.uk

Top: Thatching at St Margaret's Church, Hales, Norfolk © CCT
Bottom Right: Cultural Recovery Fund repairs and (left) conservation work at Priory Church of St Mary's, Bungay © CCT

THE FUTURE OF THE UK's CHURCH BUILDINGS

PLACES OF WORSHIP

The Future of our Churches

The Right Reverend John Arnold
Bishop of Salford

"Any church is a spiritual landmark, a witness to the Faith of the people who gather there."

There has been an uninterrupted programme for the building of churches in the British Isles, over many centuries. As populations have continued to grow, and faith has been more socially embedded, there has been a need for more buildings as places of worship and witness. This has, in turn, been accelerated by the diversity in the different Christian churches; Catholic, Anglican, Free Church, Methodists, Baptists and more.

I arrived as Bishop of Salford, in December 2014, at a rather particular moment of diocesan development. This is a Diocese about which I had previously known nothing. I arrived to find that the Diocese was entering a new chapter. For a full century and more, there had been an enormous influx of migrant workers, particularly from Ireland, as the area continued its rapid industrial development, with the opening of mines, cotton mills and factories.

There had always been a significant population of recusant Catholics, but this number was greatly increased by the newcomers. Ireland also provided large numbers of priests because vocations to the priesthood greatly exceeded the needs of the Irish Church. The existent Parishes were quickly sub-divided, and many new churches built. In 1930, there were 146 parishes.

The last fifty years has seen a reverse in this development and a decline in the church-going population and the reduction in the number of priests available for pastoral ministry. By 1980, it was already becoming clear that the Diocese had simply too many churches for the Catholic population. It was time to re-think the structure of the Diocese. A certain reduction in the number of churches had already taken place before my arrival but there was need for consultation and planning.

The COVID-19 pandemic has brought further considerations to light. Technology has been employed on a large scale to provide live streaming of liturgies available to anyone, anywhere, who has access to the internet. For one simple example, the Easter Triduum in 2020 was live streamed from St John's Cathedral, Salford, and people in over 100 countries viewed the liturgies.

Many parish priests have reported that more people have been virtually present by live-streaming, than would have been physically present in the church in normal circumstances. The question arises as to how many people have returned to churches now that restrictions on capacity are ended?

Spiritual landmarks

Any church is a spiritual landmark, a witness to the Faith of the people who gather there. The landmarks within the cities and throughout the countryside were often the church towers and steeples until the arrival of skyscrapers which now dwarf the city skyline. The churches and their ancillary buildings were not only places of worship but also centres of community life, often providing centres for youth activities and services for charitable outreach to the local community.

How important is a church? While it is certainly true that we can pray anywhere, at any time, there is an importance about that physical gathering together, sharing our prayer and liturgy in community. For Catholics, the Eucharist remains central to our sense of belonging to the One Body, who is Christ. While "spiritual communion" has purpose and value, it does not substitute the reception of the Eucharist in the celebration of Mass together. A church provides an important place for the presence of a community that gathers together to celebrate, renew, and nourish its mission.

It was important that we devised a plan for the whole of the Diocese so that all areas were to be served by the accessibility of churches and the ministry of priests. We are fortunate in that the Diocese of Salford is geographically relatively small, but it is divided into urban, suburban and rural areas. It was important that no-one should feel isolated from a church.

>>

> *"I hope that as many churches as possible can remain open and fulfilling their primary purpose."*

✝ The Future of our Churches

>>

There were the added complications that some churches are listed, while other well-maintained churches are too close to other churches or are now in areas of much-reduced population. There were difficult decisions to be made and our reasoning had to be made available and carefully explained to those affected.

While a church may be a central feature in a community, and an enduring sign and witness to faith, a redundant church can easily become a countersign, when it is allowed to decay and is left vulnerable to vandals and thieves. When a church ceases its liturgical life, there would seem to be three possible options.

Centres of social outreach

The most preferred option would be for it to become a centre of social outreach, meeting a need of that community. If seen to be continuing under Church administration, the church building can still be a powerful witness to the application of gospel values, as when it is used as a foodbank, a day centre offering advice, training and learning facilities, or even a night shelter for the homeless.

A second option is the leasing or sale of the building to a charitable organisation which allows it to remain a witness for good works even if no longer overseen by the Diocese. In such a case it is important that the sale or lease includes restrictive covenants on the building's use. People who for years might have known the building as the place for their baptisms or weddings or where the funeral of family members and friends have taken place, might be offended by its conversion to so-called profane use, such as a gymnasium, restaurant, or nightclub.

The third option is the demolition of the church building. This is always a sadness and understandable regret felt by many people who have had associations with the place, often over several generations. But it is an option that must be available.

Costs of repair

Buildings, particularly those with extensive histories, can be very expensive in their upkeep and maintenance and repair. Where there is no viable community, the cost of repair cannot be met. Demolition is preferable to dereliction and decay. I certainly dislike the thought of demolishing a church, but it is an action that must be applied in some cases. Even in such a case, care can be taken to ensure that the land is used for a good purpose, such as social housing or education.

I am left with an important principle. Jesus never established any building as a place of worship. Nor did he define the development and building of the future Church in terms of buildings. His mission was constantly in travelling and meeting people on the road, in their homes, in open spaces.

Church buildings are certainly important for us, especially for the witness they give to the faith of a community. They are important as places for gathering for prayer and sacrament and catechesis and for social outreach to the poor, the marginalised.

I hope that as many churches as possible can remain open and fulfilling their primary purpose. But we should acknowledge that, though important and loved, they are not essential to the practice and mission of our faith. Sentimental attraction is understandable and has value, but it cannot override the fundamental mission of the Church.

The Right Reverend John Arnold

The Right Reverend John Arnold is the eleventh Roman Catholic Bishop of Salford. He was formerly an auxiliary bishop of the Roman Catholic Archdiocese of Westminster and held the titular see of Lindisfarne.

www.dioceseofsalford.org.uk

"Buildings, particularly those with extensive histories, can be very expensive in their upkeep and maintenance and repair."

Left: Roman Catholic priest preparing for a wedding service © Pressfoto.co.uk / Alamy Stock Photo
Bottom: Salford Cathedral © Michael D Beckwith

PLACES OF WORSHIP

Society needs *church* buildings

Rev Lucy Winkett
Rector of St James's Church, Piccadilly in central London
and a Trustee of the National Churches Trust

"A historic and beautiful church building reminds you that you are part of a bigger story than your own life, one that spans the centuries."

As people and as a society we need church buildings. Up until the COVID-19 lockdown I'd taken it for granted. Being able to be in St James's Piccadilly, my church building, to do my job. But in March 2020 not only was I asked to close the church building to the congregation, I was also asked not to enter the church building myself, even to practise my new found skills in live-streaming.

Encouragingly, large numbers of people found us online who had never found us before. I learned to preach to a tiny dot at the top of a laptop, imagining the faces of the people watching. And as the months have gone on, after successful applications for funding to install AV equipment to ensure we can live stream, well almost everything, we are now bound to ask: what use are the buildings themselves if we can gather online and do all that we were able to do when we were there?

Tear down the temple

It's an irony that although church buildings are built for one purpose, the worship of God, it is often the people who do the worshipping who have the most ambivalent attitude towards them. Because of the emphasis in Christian theology on spiritual presence and connection, the stones of our temples are regarded with anything from guilty pleasure to downright suspicion by congregations that listen to Christ's teaching which constantly privileged people over property, actions over architecture. It's the 'tear this temple down in three days' kind of teaching that leaves some congregations wanting to sit lightly in relation to the inheritance of the buildings themselves.

But many people who do not darken the doors of a church when it's hosting what it's meant to host – worship – feel differently. For these visitors, purposely visiting at any time other than a Sunday morning, there seems to be often less ambivalence about the art and architecture and time to enjoy the space and the peace.

Therein lies a clue to the future of church buildings. They are the original 'multi-purpose spaces'. That they are still being used for their original purpose after hundreds of years or more, that generation after generation have brought their deepest griefs, their profoundest loves and their bravest hopes to a church building in funerals, weddings and christenings, is important, alongside the daily, weekly or monthly round of services that still punctuate life for many.

As well as timetabled services and worship, perhaps even more important, are the in-between times, and the in-between spaces that enrich and ennoble a human life that has a church building on its routes and in its heart.

As one of those people who is there on a Sunday, I believe that by continuing to use the building for its original purpose of worship, I help to hold a space for those who will never come then but do come when they're ready, in their own time. In theological terms, church buildings are 'penultimate': that is, bricks and mortar that point to a reality that is eternal, beyond themselves. But you don't have to sign up to that theology to appreciate the value and inspiration of a church building.

A rolling scroll of generations

A historic and beautiful church building reminds you that you are part of a bigger story than your own life, one that spans the centuries. It places you within a rolling scroll of generations whose life stories offer you the opportunity to learn, to find peace, to face the reality of death itself, to consider what you might leave behind.

>>

"To make our churches the multi-purpose public spaces they can be in a hurting world."

Society needs *church* buildings

>>

And all church buildings, ancient or modern serve as a gateway to wider society, through the other people and organisations who use the place, bringing other voices and perspectives to their lives and a sense of hope and connection.

As we emerge through the pandemic, I have been interested to see the question of whether church buildings have a future being debated in a way that is not the case for other buildings such as theatres, pubs, concert halls or schools. The people who use and run these buildings are not saying that live performance and in-person experience can be replicated online; rather they can't wait for them to reopen

We need church buildings

The truth is that as people and as a society we need church buildings. At their best, they are public spaces with low barriers to entry (thresholds), that are open just because they're open, free and easy to enter, inclusive, adaptable, beautiful, with a strong tradition of connection across time and space. For a population exhausted by isolation, tired of looking at screens, confined very often to a small flat or a room; the spacious high-roof of a church building can elevate the spirits as much as the much-needed green spaces did when we were confined to one walk a day.

Of course, some Church of England buildings are in the wrong places for a population that has been moving since the Industrial Revolution, with people leaving behind small towns and villages. But post-Covid, the word is that people are moving out of cities again. If that proves to be a lasting change let's seize the challenge; as well as bringing new people into these churches for worship, church buildings can be used for live music, for good conversation, for debate or for learning and could provide the centre for a community where the post office or pub closed long ago.

Church buildings tell stories about our lives and our society, and stories matter. To tell the histories of these islands n such a way that commits to a just society in the present. To lead on creating environmentally friendly spaces, to help our society face the contested history of our past, a vital and urgent task. Maya Angelou wrote that 'history despite its wrenching pain cannot be unlived. But if faced with courage, need not be lived again'. A manifesto for the opening, interpretation and welcoming of visitors to every historic church building in the land.

For many church buildings, to be the welcoming clear-eyed story tellers that they can be in a community, what is actually needed is quite simple: volunteers, good toilets, decent heating and a roof that doesn't leak, together with a vision that proclaims that these buildings matter, not just to the Church but to the society they serve. To make our churches the multi-purpose public spaces they can be in a hurting world that has never needed them more, those considerations are a great place to start.

Rev Lucy Winkett

Lucy Winkett has been the Rector of St James's Church, Piccadilly since 2010. Her early ordained ministry was spent at St Paul's Cathedral, London, where she was a minor canon and chaplain and the canon precentor. She is a Trustee of the National Churches Trust.

Top: All Saints Church, Old Buckenham, Norfolk © Saul Penfold
Bottom: Parish celebration © Diocese of Westminster

PLACES OF WORSHIP

Bringing *people* together

By Rev Eve Pitts and Anthony Pitts
Holy Trinity Church, Birchfield, Birmingham

"People identify with church buildings, even if they do not often attend services. The church is there for people who need them, for life's important rites of passage. Some families identify with churches for generations for this purpose."

The meaning of 'church' in the Bible is the group of believers in Christ who met in each other's homes. But today when we hear the word 'church' we think of a building which is needed for Christian worship.

Church buildings are important for they enable Christians to worship together. They were built as a response to God, to enable Christians to worship together in larger numbers than a home will allow.

Church buildings are important in that they provided a consistent meeting place for Christians, often with a capacity of a hundred or more. They are a place set aside; they are seen as special; they are a sacred space to which we come with respect and reverence.

Church buildings speak of permanence, stability and serenity. They can serve as places to withdraw to from the hectic, over-busy and anxious times we live in. They can be places where people come when they feel tired, to find rest and peace.

At the heart of communities

In addition to their role as places of worship, church buildings are valuable resources for the whole community, used and cherished by people regardless of their religion. Church buildings are still very much at the heart of communities.

Church buildings, especially attractive old ones, are important because people find the symbolism and the craftmanship attractive and comforting. It suggests something permanent and transcendent; it links with the past. It transcends daily life.

Church buildings are important because they proclaim that God is present and active in the world, and that God is not to be forgotten. It is sometimes difficult to put into words, but churches bring out respect and loyalty in people, and a sense of the sacred.

For people who need them

Churches can subtly create within people a sense of the divine in conscious and unconscious ways. They provide places for silence and calm, reflection and prayer. Architecture is important: attractive church buildings can transmit something of the character of the Christian faith as well as the perception that this building is special – a place where God can be encountered.

People identify with church buildings, even if they do not often attend services. The church is there for people who need them, for life's important rites of passage. Some families identify with churches for generations for this purpose.

They are seen as 'our church' in our neighbourhood. They are always there, and have always been there, so it seems. The physical presence of a church is a symbol of the permanency of the culture in which people live their lives. They are a cultural resource.

>>

Bringing the community together © Diocese of Westminster

Bringing *people* together

\>\>

The centre of social life

Many church buildings are important because they are multi-purpose, enabling meetings of different kinds, such as schools or lunch clubs. In a small place a church might be the centre of social life, especially when other buildings such as public houses and shops have closed.

Church buildings are usually seen as safe places for those in need or in crisis, whether or not the people in need are Christians.

Church buildings are important because people go to them for spiritual 'repair'. They can provide answers that no other places offer. In urban areas, church buildings can bring people together from different backgrounds for prayer and worship.

Rev Eve Pitts and Anthony Pitts

Rev Eve Pitts was ordained as a deacon in 1989 and in 1994 was one of the first black women ordained a priest in the Church of England. In 2010 she moved to Holy Trinity church in the inner city parish of Birchfield, Birmingham where she has led a major programme of repairs which have led to the church being removed from the Heritage at Risk Register.

www.holytrinity-church.co.uk

Top: **Children's activity at St Stephen's church, Bowling, Bradford**
Bottom: **Holy Trinity Church, Birchfield, Birmingham** © Holy Trinity Church

THE FUTURE OF THE UK's CHURCH BUILDINGS

PLACES OF WORSHIP

The Great Good Place

Rev Canon John McGinley
Executive Director, Myriad

> *"We will need to create church and do mission in the third spaces in which people already gather – the gym, care home, community centre."*

"I prefer our shed church Mummy" said seven year-old Sam to his mother Catherine as they left one of our nation's finest cathedrals after a morning service. The 'shed church' he was referring to was the building of St John the Baptist church, Hinckley, Leicestershire where I was vicar.

Catherine had come to faith in Christ a few years earlier and Sam and his sister had started to attend services as her faith came alive. Sam's statement was very perceptive as St John's had been erected in the 1950s using the design of an agricultural building with the intention of constructing a "proper" church once the new daughter church congregation had been established. We were now in 2006 and no proper church building had been constructed, and the 'shed' was now deteriorating as it had exceeded its fifty year life expectancy.

Sam's experience reveals a number of the key aspects of our relationship with church buildings today. Firstly it is a story of mission and salvation. He and his family had come to faith in Christ at St John's Church because of the holiday club, social events, children's work and Alpha Course that all played a part in their journey to faith.

That required a building that could host these events and despite its poor shed-like appearance the flexible seating, kitchen and video screen were key in this. The church in the United Kingdom is in a missionary, post-Christendom and post Christian context. Only seven percent of the population regularly engage in Christian worship. The result of this is that our buildings have to serve a missionary purpose and not only provide facilities for worship.

Sam's conversation is also instructive because he wasn't expressing a preference for sheds over gothic cathedrals, he was expressing how the experience of friendship and church family, the participatory form of worship and the engaging activities were what was meaningful for him. But at the same time his reference to the 'shed' also shows that he had a relationship with the physical building, that he was aware of his surroundings and that nothing could hide the fact that it was like meeting in a shed!

As human beings God has made us with spatial awareness and an appreciation of form and colour, where the environment in which we live has a significant impact upon us. We connect spaces with experiences and we differentiate buildings according to what happens in them. Therefore, the physical environment in which missionary activity takes place can be significant in a person's journey to faith.

One way of understanding how people relate to church buildings is as 'third places'. This phrase comes from Ray Oldenburg's assessment of the spaces in which we live our lives in his book The Great Good Place, with home and our immediate household classified as the first place, our work place, or educational establishment, is the second and then there are third places.

Church buildings are examples of third places, and so are coffee shops, social or sports clubs, public libraries, parks and gyms. These places are homes from home, where we can relax with others in public, where we experience community and they act as another anchor point for our lives.

Open and readily accessible to everyone

From Oldenburg's recognition of the significance of third places we can see how important church buildings can be for people. And this has so much missional potential as we invite people into our church buildings to explore faith. But third place thinking also reveals the challenge of making church buildings places of mission because third places in our culture have certain characteristics which people look for as they look to find those homes from home. They must be open and readily accessible to everyone. They need to be hospitable and comfortable for those who are there. The mood and tone is one of informality, with nothing pretentious or grandiose; they have a homely feel.

>>

"The physical environment of a church building… has a big effect on whether people feel like this is a place they can be at home."

The Great Good Place

>>

We can recognise this description in our high street coffee shops or gyms, but how many of our church buildings can be described like this? Our buildings were designed to inspire people to worship God when they were built. But to people in our culture they can often feel cold, austere, and unwelcoming, and they often lack the facilities to enable accessibility and hospitality. The physical environment of a church building, into which people are invited, has a big effect on whether they feel like this is a place they can be at home.

It is for all these reasons that I lead Myriad, a team of people with a vision for encouraging churches to replant and revitalise churches in existing church buildings or to plant churches in different spaces. In my twenty-six years of ordained ministry I have been involved in four church building projects; the redevelopment of two Grade II listed Victorian buildings and the demolition of two deteriorating twentieth century buildings and the reconstruction of new church and community spaces. But I have also worshipped and prayed, spoken at evangelistic events and led enquirers courses in pubs, coffee shops, local parks and school halls.

Creating church in the third spaces in which people already gather

I am convinced that we need a 'both and' not an 'either or' approach to deciding how church buildings can serve the church's mission and whether to plant in a new location. Every building and community is unique and each one will need a different approach. Some of the buildings will be heritage buildings that inspire a connection with the awe and wonder of God and should be used for worship, significant festival and civic events. To try and redesign the building is not possible or economically practical so alongside them we will need to create church and do mission in the third spaces in which people already gather – the gym, care home, community centre.

Other church buildings have potential to have aspects of them redeveloped for mission and doing so maximises the potential of the social capital in people's memory of the church, and appreciation for the church's role in the local community. But for them to become third places in people's lives there will need to be places within them where people can relax, with facilities to serve them. And the 'both and' approach will enable us to think creatively about what aspects of church life and mission should take place in which places. And with the pandemic development of online facilities the church as a third place will also involve digital communities and 'spaces'.

I am so glad that in the 1950's the people of Holy Trinity Church, Hinckley had the vision to plant a daughter church and build a 'shed' to host the community of St John's Church. It has meant that hundreds of people like Catherine and Sam have come to faith in Jesus Christ. We will need such courage and creativity as we respond to the missionary challenges of our time and discern how our church buildings and other places can play their part.

Rev Canon John McGinley

Rev Canon John McGinley is Executive Director, Myriad and of The Gregory Centre for Church Multiplication.

Top: The new St John's church, **Hinckley** © Nigel May
Centre: The 1950's church
Bottom: Grace Church, Highlands in north London which began as a church plant from Christ Church, Cockfosters © CCX

COMMUNITY

In-Spire-d to make Music

Barbara Eifler
Chief Executive, Making Music

making music
SUPPORTING AND CHAMPIONING LEISURE-TIME MUSIC

"Music groups have long cherished churches as spaces for rehearsal and performance."

Churches and leisure-time music groups have much in common: despite the one usually having striking architectural features punctuating the landscape and the other making quite a lot of noise, both are frequently not noticed as they go about their daily business.

It is only when you are looking for a place to rehearse your orchestra, band or choir that you suddenly see churches everywhere. And only when searching for a choir or an event near you that you realise how much is happening musically right on your doorstep.

So do these two surprisingly invisible giants of all communities know and help each other become more visible? We believe they do.

'We' are Making Music, the UK association for leisure-time music, with over 3,600 music groups in membership, comprising around 200,000 hobby musicians. Impressive numbers, but the (limited) data suggests we only represent about 26% of all adult music groups in the UK.

Making Music offers its members practical support for running their group. Most are small charities managed by a committee of volunteers. We help them navigate everything from writing safeguarding policies to claiming Gift Aid, designing effective posters to setting up a Twitter account, recruiting new participants or finding a leader for their choir. There are artistic development opportunities, such as our Adopt a Music Creator project.

We also connect groups to each other, to relevant experts, services and suppliers, and to new potential audiences and participants. And as the largest leisure-time music organisation, we act as a voice for the sector.

58% of concerts will take place in churches

Around 60% are choirs; 30% instrumental groups – from brass bands to amateur orchestras, ukulele groups to handbell ringers – and the other 10% are amateur promoters, that is, they present professional soloists or small ensembles in concert, but they are doing so as volunteers, not to earn a living.

These groups usually operate all year round, offering a wide range of music, from pop to classical music, folk to jazz, world music to brass band repertoire.

The amateur promoters will host an average of seven concerts a year (so for those in our membership, a total of about 6,000 events annually), to audiences of around 385,000. 58% of their concerts will take place in churches.

Our performing groups – vocal or instrumental – will also stage concerts, an average of 3.8 a year; including other kinds of events (e.g. Come and Sing Days or workshops) that totals around 24,000 annually. Their concert audiences are around 1.5 million people a year and 70% of their events take place in churches.

But our performing groups' main activity is their regular rehearsal, usually weekly. Public events give these rehearsals a focus or goal, but the practising together in itself is of great benefit to participants and for many a highlight of their weekly routine, as I can personally attest: having started learning the trumpet three years ago for a fundraising challenge, I then joined a brass band. Concentrating for 90 minutes on playing the right notes melts away the stresses of the day and there is almost physical comfort in the harmonies we create and experience together. How did I cope before band?

\>\>

THE FUTURE OF THE UK's CHURCH BUILDINGS

In-Spire-d to make Music

"Churches and leisure-time music groups have much in common."

>>

Here's some of the reasons churches are so popular as rehearsal or performance spaces with our music groups:

- There is one in every community! Being geographically accessible is really important – you want to be able to get quickly to your weekly music fix and enjoy it with people who live nearby.

- Churches are large! There are not many buildings spacious enough to accommodate a 200 strong community choir or a full-size (usually about 85 people) amateur symphony orchestra, including large instruments such as percussion, harps or double basses.

- Churches are affordable! Other similarly large spaces would be far too expensive for these music groups: they fund themselves mostly by subscriptions from their own members, subscriptions they want to keep low in order to enable anyone and everyone to join. This 'public benefit' thinking chimes well ethically with churches' focus on supporting their communities.

- Churches are beautiful! Many people no longer visit them for religious worship, but nonetheless cherish the buildings and want to experience, admire and support them – for example by paying weekly rent for music rehearsals or buying a ticket for a concert.

- Many churches having been built well before the microphone was an affordable accessory to all, they also tend to have great acoustics.

There are a few potential improvements suggested by groups now and then…

Ventilation, in Covid-times, might be A Good Thing, but it's hard to enjoy music or a practise session in a draft and without heating.

Toilets. Are there any? Or enough? A rehearsal session or concert will be 1.5 to 2 hours long, and the organisers will arrive earlier and leave later, so facilities are essential. A lack of them can be off putting for audiences, especially as around two-thirds of them are aged 50+; intervals can be difficult to manage.

Is your building accessible to all kinds of people of all ages or disabilities? 18% of the population, that's 12 million people, have a disability, and over state pension age it is one in two people. Making your building welcoming to music groups and their audiences also means your congregation and wider community are able to join in with worship and the many other activities you may be hosting throughout a week.

Music groups have long cherished churches as spaces for rehearsal and performance, and churches have found that this regular activity contributes significantly to their income and perhaps also enriches their summer fêtes, and accompanies their weddings, baptisms or funerals.

A match made on earth – we hope you continue to support each other and flourish as the architectural and musical cornerstones of your communities.

Barbara Eifler FRSA

Barbara Eifler has extensive experience of running arts membership organisations, including the Stage Management Association, of which she was Executive Director for 12 years. An amateur musician herself, and with 25 years of experience in arts-related charities, Barbara is well versed in the issues facing voluntary musicians and music groups.

www.makingmusic.org.uk

Top: Calne Choral Society performing Mozart's Requiem at St Andrew's Church, Chippenham © Making Music
Middle left: Big Noise Chorus © Making Music
Middle right: Sheffield Philharmonic Orchestra rehearsing at Victoria Hall, a Methodist place of worship.
Bottom right: Ionian Clarinet Choir rehearsing © Making Music

THE FUTURE OF THE UK's CHURCH BUILDINGS

COMMUNITY

Helping *to fight* hunger

Simon Thomson
Head of Communications
FareShare

"Church buildings offer a safe, warm and affordable location."

FareShare is the UK's longest running food redistribution charity. We were born out of the belief that no good food should go to waste, especially when people are going hungry. This belief is as central to our work now as it was when we started more than 25 years ago.

Hundreds of the charities and community groups we support across the UK operate out of churches and other places of worship. These organisations play a vital role in their local communities, just like the venues they rely on, helping vulnerable people with much needed care and support.

Church buildings offer a safe, warm and affordable location for these groups, which have limited funds, and need to make sure they spend every penny they can on the people they support.

One of the churches we work with is Marpool URC, in Heanor, Amber Valley, East Midlands. Based in an old mining town, now a market town, the relatively new church building is wheelchair friendly and has a disabled toilet with baby changing facilities and is a hub for belonging, open to the whole community. More than two-thirds of the users of the premises do not belong to the congregation.

During the pandemic the church set up a Covid-19 foodbank. People receive weekly food parcels, either picked up from the church building or home-delivered. The food mainly comes from FareShare (supplemented with personal donations and a local supermarket) and is bagged up and distributed from the church building. During the last 12 months, around 2,300 parcels have been made.

Foodbanks

One foodbank user, a young single women, said: 'The foodbank has helped me when I have had absolutely nothing; and has taught me to make meals with little ingredients, for if I am skint in the future. I think I will be using the service for the next few months as I have suffered with terrible mental health and require rehab in the next upcoming months due to alcohol addiction. Once again, I want to say thank you. I really don't know what I would do: at times it's scary and you guys really do help: just having a bit of food in the cupboard…it is a comforting feeling.'

When the churches FareShare works with were closed during lockdown, it wasn't just congregations that were affected, but also people relying on this community-based care and support. During the height of the pandemic, FareShare worked with these charities, and thousands more like them, to provide food parcels to those who otherwise would have gone without.

We wanted to help those in need

Gateway Church Foodbank, which has been supporting people in Barnsley with food parcels to help them through tough times, since 2013 was one of these.

Stephanie Aplin-Wakefield from Gateway Church Foodbank told me: "We're a church and one of our leaders had it in her heart do more than just preach, and wanted to help those that were in need – so one of those ways was to feed them.

"Right from the beginning of the pandemic, we have stayed open. At the first lockdown it was just Pastor Mark and I running things. We had to do everything by phone and email, and we were doing deliveries. Now, we're no longer doing deliveries, as we are feeding 100-130 people per week, so there's just not enough time to deliver as well.

"We're seeing a real mixture of people, from asylum seekers, homeless people, housing association, people with mental health issues, those on probation, community midwives refer families. We're also working with organisations like Christians Against Poverty and Citizens Advice."

>>

> *"One of our leaders had it in her heart to do more than just preach, and wanted to help those that were in need – so one of those ways was to feed them."*

Helping *fight* hunger

"We realise it's not just about feeding people, we've got to feed the mind too. So if people are struggling with their mental health, figuring out why and helping them move forward. If someone is homeless, why are they homeless? If they've lost their job or they're ill, what can we do to help? This is our future project under the umbrella, mind, body and soul."

A third example of how churches work to help local people who are struggling is Christ Church in Barnet, London. The church launched its foodbank more than eight years ago to provide much needed items to those most in need and they currently support around 15 households in the local area.

Mobilising local people

Jean Corney from the foodbank explained to me how the church can mobilise local people: "We're a parish church with a school attached and they have been very good at collecting food for us. The headmistress is very supportive, we get lovely harvest donations from them and once a term they ask what we need. The parents are also very supportive – those supplies have kept us going."

"We have also received generous support in addition from three other schools and have been delighted by support from the local Rotary group and those living in the streets around who follow our foodbank Facebook page and astound us each week with their donations."

The church has continued to provide food parcels to people throughout the pandemic, delivering direct to people at home.

"What is lovely is that you can add dignity back by giving people choices – we can say 'here's what we've had from Waitrose, what would you like?' The atmosphere is more pleasant for people coming in which is a huge bonus. Both Waitrose stores have been very supportive, and we got money through the green token collections – that was a huge boost!"

Of course, as well as churches, FareShare works with many other people and organisations ranging from banks, food companies and local authorities. But churches provide many of the spaces needed for those helping us in our work in cities, towns and villages and are supported by volunteers who know their local area well and are motivated to help those in need.

Church buildings are essential local buildings and we certainly need them so that we can continue to work in partnership with local charities and organisations helping to fight hunger in the UK.

Simon Thomson

Simon Thomson works to communicate the work of FareShare, the UK's largest food redistribution charity, sending surplus food from the food industry through a network of more than 10,500 charities and community groups across the UK.

www.fareshare.org.uk

Top: Soup a lunch
Below: Helping provide food during COVID-19 (left) © Sanktus Volunteers/Our Lady Help of Christians
Food at Marpool United Reformed Church (right)

COMMUNITY

The *communal* benefits of sacred space

Dominic Grieve
QC

> *"Seeing sacred space sensitively married to effective community use is always a delight. The building lives and memory is joined to the present."*

Our churches and chapels in the UK are as varied as the history of our Christian faith. A few are filled for services on a Sunday, but many are three quarters empty and some may always have been so. Some are modern but others an architectural amalgam of centuries of development and occasionally semi-ruin.

They cost a lot to maintain and they do not necessarily lend themselves to modern styles of worship. Many are only used for few hours a week, even if an attached church hall may be much busier with community activity such as clubs, scouts and nursery schools and may indeed provide the main source of income for upkeep.

Yet it is the sacred space of the building itself and the communal memory it contains that defines it. Without it the adjacent hall is no more than another "public facility". And despite the decline in the quantity of organised Christian religion that is the hallmark of our age, there is still a need for accessible and benign sacred space.

This is noticeable in the presence of individuals who will enter a church, if open, to sit in it for silent reflection or walk round it and take an interest in its content as a place of memory and often artistic beauty. It is also the case that those who want to use what it offers at key moments of life or find comfort from its physical presence and use as a community hub, where the faith based foundations of its management are perhaps counter intuitively a reassurance and an attraction and not a deterrent to coming over the threshold.

Covid lockdown

This became particularly apparent to me during the Covid lockdown. For the congregation, digital worship for those who attend my 1950's London church provided important but limited attractions, but numbers revived completely once the bar on "in person" services was lifted.

But more strikingly the presence of the church, in ringing the tolling bell for the Duke of Edinburgh's funeral or the decision to sing our one permitted congregational hymn in the churchyard at the end of the service against the background of a busy main road attracted nothing but favourable comment from passers-by.

The weekly mother and toddlers group uses the church nave with its robust wooden benches, as does the brass band which appreciates the acoustic for rehearsals, as does the Thursday friendship group open to all. The hundreds who attended our last Christmas carol service which is run with the help of the same brass band, the use of the churchyard for selling Christmas trees and the musical events that draw people in, show that the benefits offered are far beyond the existence of a hall for letting.

In France where I have a holiday home, the law of 1906 effectively nationalised all earlier church buildings, turning the congregations into licensees. As the French State struggles to pay for the fabric, you can all too often feel the neglect as you wander round, with tired fittings and furnishings and a feeling of it all being rather unloved; often cold and damp.

Even when the church is being used for concerts and cultural purposes as well as worship there is a sense of lack of ownership and care, unless it is of national importance as a building. Sometimes they feel semi-secularised and lifeless, despite being in good repair.

Restoring and maintaining churches

This is why think there is so much that can be achieved in our country by helping existing congregations to restore and maintain their churches and chapels and develop their use for local communities whilst respecting their primary purpose as sacred space. Far from making that community use more difficult, I am convinced that the recognition of that primary purpose facilitates it and makes it much more relevant to users.

Obviously challenges and opportunities differ widely from one part of the country to another. The scope for projects in a deeply rural area is not the same as in an inner city. But as long as there is a congregation wanting and willing to worship and to participate and work for community benefit, then the platform is there for caring for the building and maximising its usage.

>>

Coming together for worship © Diocese of Westminster

The *communal* benefits of sacred space

>>

In the process you can achieve far more than the preservation of historic buildings. You can help sustain and restore community life. You don't do that by closing, much less demolishing, the church building.

When I am driving around the country, I can't resist stopping to look at the churches which I pass. If by good fortune they are not locked, and most are usually open, then ten minutes of visit tells one a lot, not just about their architecture and history but also about current use.

Seeing sacred space sensitively married to effective community use is always a delight. The building lives and memory is joined to the present. It is the outcome we should be working for as it offers a far better contribution to our common good than mere preservation no matter how well written the explanatory leaflet.

With the help of organisations like the National Churches Trust we, in our church and chapel communities, should be able to persuade donors that this is a cause worthy of being further taken forward.

Dominic Grieve

Dominic Grieve is a barrister and served as Shadow Home Secretary from 2008 to 2009 and Attorney General for England and Wales from 2010 to 2014. He served as the Member of Parliament for Beaconsfield from 1997 to 2019.

Top: A Post office in St James' church, West Hampstead © GraingePhotography
Bottom: Restaurant in St Giles' Parish Church Pontefract, Yorkshire © St Giles' church

THE FUTURE OF THE UK's CHURCH BUILDINGS

COMMUNITY

Churches *in the* pandemic

Rt Hon Stephen Timms MP
Chair, All Party Parliamentary Group
on Faith and Society

"In 2020, it was the faith groups, and the churches in particular, which uniquely had both the motivation and the capacity to support communities through the crisis."

The All Party Parliamentary Group on Faith and Society was set up in 2012 to draw attention to the very positive contributions faith groups and faith-based organisations are making in communities all over the country. We wanted also, where we could, to help remove barriers which have often made it hard for them to fulfill their potential.

We began to meet faith-based organisations and to discuss how they were finding things. We quickly learned that many were struggling in their relationship with the local Council. Councils are very familiar with working with voluntary sector organisations, including commissioning services from them. But many have been reluctant to work with faith groups.

Councils worry that working with faith groups will cause problems. Some fear the groups will only really be interested in converting people. Or, if they do provide a service, it will be biased in favour of members of that group. In practice, as far as I can tell, neither of these problems ever actually occurs. But it is possible they might. And some are very eager to whip up anxiety about them.

That all changed in 2020. It came home to me that something had changed on Good Friday. I was sitting at home that morning, looking through some emails, and I came across two from constituents saying: "I don't have any food. What should I do?"

Of course, over the past ten years, I have become very familiar with referring people to foodbanks. But they would all be shut over the Easter holiday weekend, so I didn't know how to reply. However, I looked further back through my inbox, and found an email from the Mayor of Newham, Rokhsana Fiaz. It said: if you come across people without food over the holiday weekend, you should email the Vicar of Ascension Church, Royal Docks before 10 in the morning. He will then arrange for a food parcel to be delivered later that day.

I didn't have any better ideas, so I tried it. Both my constituents received their food parcels.

My local Council has never worked seriously with faith groups before. It was clear that something unusual was going on.

Keeping the faith

Our APPG carried out a research project with Goldsmith's, University of London, over the Summer of 2020. A questionnaire was sent to every local Council in the UK. Almost half replied, and their responses showed that collaboration between Councils and faith groups has dramatically increased in the pandemic, and especially with churches. The report of the research is called "Keeping the Faith". 60% of local councils told us that they had been working with church-based foodbanks during the pandemic.

In some ways, more striking still than that was the very positive experiences council officers reported of these collaborations. One told the researcher: "My personal admiration for faith groups has gone through the roof, just in terms of their commitment there. We as a local authority didn't know what we were getting into. And they have got involved with smiles on their faces and they have done it professionally."

>>

"Collaboration between Councils and faith groups has dramatically increased in the pandemic, and especially with churches."

Churches in the pandemic

\>\>

The researchers put to the local authorities a list of characteristics and asked whether each characterised their experience to "a great extent". "some extent", "not very much", "not at all", or "don't know". Positive characteristics scored very highly:

- "Adding value because of their longstanding presence in the local community" – 60% said that was the case " to a great extent".
- "Improving access to hard to reach groups" – 40% said that was the case "to a great extent", and another 39% "to some extent".

And the researchers also asked about negative aspects said to characterise working with faith groups.

- "Expressing socially conservative views which sit uneasily with our equalities obligations" – just 2% of the Councils said that was the case to a great extent; and
- "Causing us concern about the possibility of proselytization in the context of partnership working" – that was just 1%.

Motivation and capacity

Something very significant changed last year. We have become familiar over decades with regular reports of declining church attendance. Some believe that, given time, religious faith will die out altogether. And yet, it turned out that, in Britain in 2020, it was the faith groups, and the churches in particular, which uniquely had both the motivation and the capacity to support communities through the crisis. Far from being on the way out, they were the only players in the field. No other network or grouping or organisations came anywhere near.

And our research suggests local authorities – and I think regional and national authorities too – are not going to forget that lesson. They want these collaborations to develop and to be extended in the future.

Rt Hon Stephen Timms MP

Stephen Timms served as Chief Secretary to the Treasury from 2006 to 2007. He has been Member of Parliament for East Ham, formerly Newham North East, since 1994.

www.faithandsociety.org

Top: The Trinity Centre, Manor Park, London
Bottom: St Barnabas Church, Little Ilford, London

THE FUTURE OF THE UK's CHURCH BUILDINGS

COMMUNITY

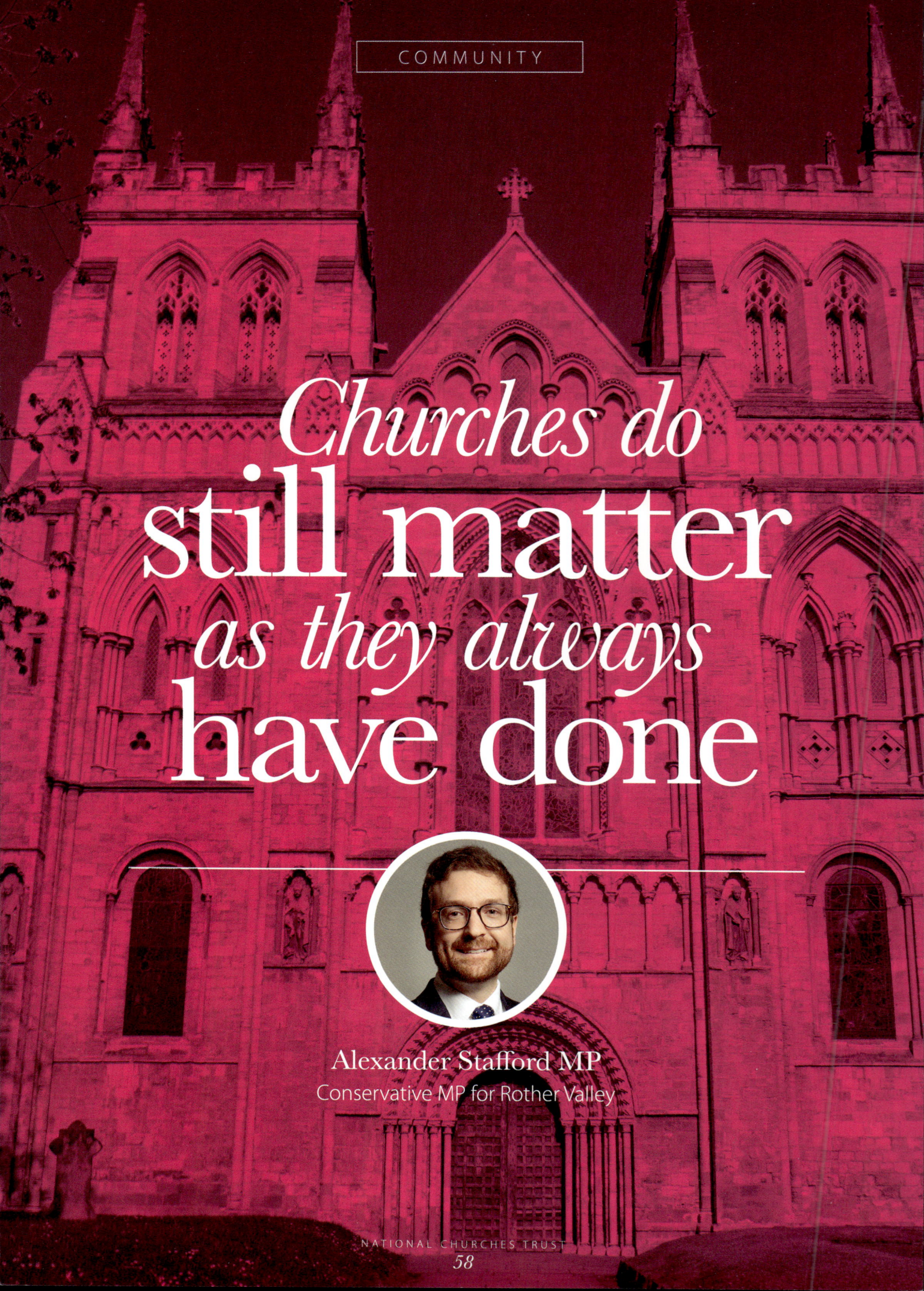

Churches do still matter *as they always* have done

Alexander Stafford MP
Conservative MP for Rother Valley

> *"Churches offer something to everyone, believer and non-believer alike, with the positive impact on individuals and on society immeasurable."*

In the wake of the devastating coronavirus pandemic, Britain's magnificent churches proved their worth as food for the soul in these uncertain modern times. The social, economic, historical, cultural, architectural, and spiritual worth of our 39,800 churches is self-evident. Yet, now more than ever, they are facing a grave struggle to ensure their survival.

As a Roman Catholic and as a historian, I have spent much of my life sitting at a pew gazing up at various consecrated interiors: at the hammerbeam roof of my Benedictine school's abbey, at the stained-glass windows of my university chapel, and most importantly at the hanging crucifix in my local parish church. Whenever I travel, I find myself seeking out chapels, churches, abbeys, cathedrals, and basilicas of all shapes and sizes – it is an enduring interest of mine.

A reassuring constant in an ever-changing world

My abiding love for churches is born of the very same reasons that keep them relevant to life in Britain today. They are the bedrock of our society; past, present, and future. They are a living, breathing record of who we are as a people and where we have come from, spanning across the ages and connecting us with our ancestors and our descendants to come. They have borne witness to all the great events in our country's history; our triumphs, our tragedies, and foundational moments which altered the path of this nation. They also serve as a reassuring constant in an ever-changing world.

After all, there is nowhere quite like a church. It can be a place of solitude and quiet reflection from the hustle and bustle of the outside world; a source of solace and comfort as an antidote to grief; a refuge and provider of support in times of hardship; a hive of community and companionship in situations of common purpose; and a haven of tranquillity and peace for those seeking God.

In my mind, the value of our churches simply cannot be overstated. There is, of course, the spiritual nourishment that flows from Christian worship in a church – increasingly important in an irreligious age. However, churches offer something to everyone, believer and non-believer alike, with the positive impact on individuals and on society immeasurable.

Our churches are an inclusive, multi-generational space, welcoming the young, the old, the disabled, the weak, and the vulnerable equally. They are located at the hearts of our communities and are there for the people who want and need them. These versatile buildings can be used for various activities, ranging from music and the arts to youth groups and foodbanks.

This utility not only brings countless economic benefits but also shows the wisdom of partially repurposing these awe-inspiring buildings so that we can simultaneously preserve them for their original use. If we are not flexible and creative regarding the future of our churches, in many cases they will wither and die.

The architectural value and geographical spread of our churches is truly something to behold. They run the gamut from the Saxon and Norman period to the Tudor, Victorian, and modern age, ranging in type and size from the smallest chapels to the mightiest cathedrals. We have inner city concrete megachurches and City of London ancient chancels, but we also have idyllic, bucolic English country spires and windswept island outposts. Cities, towns, villages, and the countryside are all represented. The architectural and touristic draw is understandably magnetic, resulting in a clear economic gain.

>>

If we allow these spaces to disappear, they will never return and we shall regret it deeply. We must not and we will not allow this to happen.

Churches do still matter *as they always* have done

\>\>

Our churches stand testament to Britain's Christian history and heritage

Culturally, our churches are a microcosm of our society, reflecting the denominational diversity of Christian worship and belief across our United Kingdom. From the Methodism of the coal mining regions of South Yorkshire and Wales and the Anglicanism of the shires, to the Presbyterianism of Scotland and Northern Ireland, our churches stand testament to Britain's Christian history and heritage.

This has been augmented by the different groups which have made Britain their home, with Protestantism, including Baptists and Pentecostalists, strengthened by Commonwealth immigration from Africa and the West Indies, and Roman Catholicism experiencing explosive growth from successive waves of Irish, Italian, and Polish arrivals who supplemented the existing English recusants. In many senses, in addition to being a witness to our past, our churches are our modern United Kingdom.

It is natural to ask what the future holds for our British churches at a time when they are feeling the squeeze like never before. If we allow these spaces to disappear, they will never return and we shall regret it deeply. We must not and we will not allow this to happen.

We know that the need amongst the younger generation for the services provided by our churches has not gone away – the huge focus on mindfulness and self-care is evidence enough. We must harness this desire by positioning our churches as places which can cater for these needs well into the future. Churches do still matter as they always have done, and they will continue to be beacons of hope for community cohesion, belief, and heritage for many hundreds of years to come..

Alexander Stafford MP

Alexander Stafford is the Conservative MP for Rother Valley. His election in December 2019 marked the first time the seat had been won by a non-Labour candidate since the constituency's creation in 1918. In Parliament, he champions the green recovery, having previously worked for WWF and Shell. As a member of the BEIS Select Committee, chair of the ESG APPG, vice-chair of the Hydrogen APPG, and vice-chair of the Critical Minerals APPG, he is a leading voice for the role of hydrogen, green finance, ESG, and critical minerals in Britain's drive to reach net zero and to level up communities across the country. Alexander also has a deep policy interest in freedom of religion and belief and in Christianity at home and abroad.

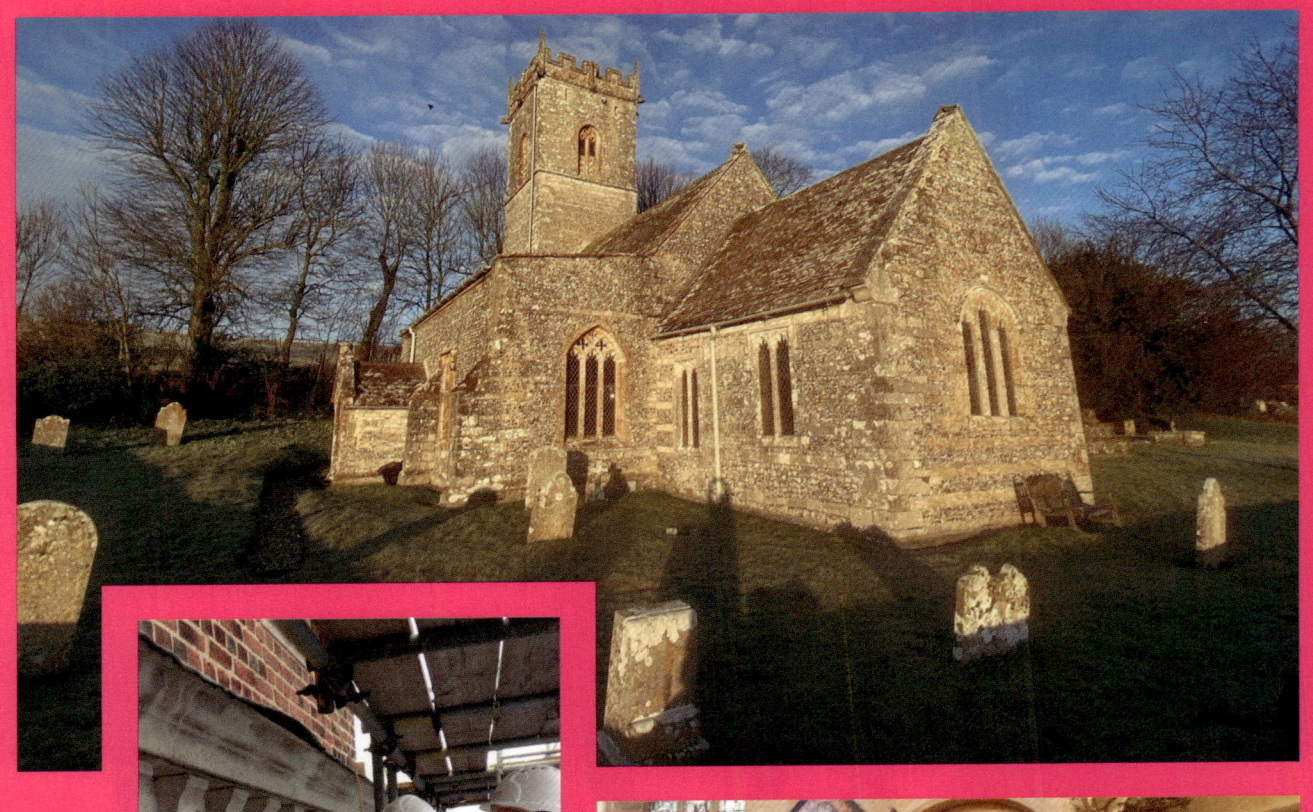

Top: St Martin's church, Cheselbourne, Dorset
Middle left: Repairs at St Mary and Holy Trinity, Bow Common
Middle right: St Mary's church, Horncastle, Lincolnshire
Bottom: Communities at an international service © Diocese of Westminster

THE FUTURE OF THE UK's CHURCH BUILDINGS

THE UNITED KINGDOM

Go thy Way

Christopher Catling
Secretary of the Royal Commission on the
Ancient and Historical Monuments of Wales

NATIONAL CHURCHES TRUST

> *"The best collections of woodwork, sculpture, and stained glass to survive in Wales outside a museum are in churches and chapels."*

I completely understand the arguments of many Christians that the maintenance and repair of historic buildings forms no part of their mission. Jesus did not command his followers to worry about raising the money to repair the gutters or pay for the heating.

On the contrary, he offered the disciples a minimalist and highly practical suggestion: 'where two or three are gathered together in my name, there am I in the midst of them' (Matthew 18:20). Arguably, then, worshipping by Zoom in order to sell churches and use the proceeds to help the homeless, the hungry, the lonely and the sick is the best way of fulfilling the teachings of Christ.

Heritage professionals like me will object, of course: 'you have no right', we will say, 'to dispose of a building that was built and paid for by the community as a whole. It is wrong that one generation should make decisions that over-ride the love and care that has gone into cherishing these buildings over many generations'.

Churches are significant repositories of community history; they contain rare and precious objects; they are, in a very real sense, places where the past is kept alive at the heart of every community. They are also places of reflection and spiritual sustenance for many more people than those who attend Sunday worship.

'Fine', says the churchgoer. 'If that's your view, how about contributing to the cost?'

Arguments like these are no doubt familiar to readers of this collection of essays. How then do we move on from the stalemate of polarised arguments, pitting heritage values against ethical and theological ones, both sides being very aware of the prodigious annual cost of maintaining these historic buildings and equally aware that no government or lottery is going to open the coffers and provide the enough money to do so?

Independent congregations are merging

I have a number of suggestions. First, we have to accept that some degree of closure is inevitable. This is a Europe-wide phenomenon, but one that is especially acute in Wales because of the large number of late 19th and early 20th-century places of worship built by independent congregations, many of which are now merging and selling off surplus buildings.

We can't save them all, but we can at least make a record of a very significant part of the lives of the people of Wales in an age when Sunday meant chapel not shopping. Make a record – that sounds simple enough – so why are we not just getting on with it?

That's because there is no central body to review and manage disposals and as few of these buildings are listed, there is no way of knowing in advance which buildings are most at risk. In Wales we depend for our intelligence on close contact with such conservation bodies as the Friends of Friendless Churches and on scouring estate agents' websites on a regular basis. Too often the first we know of a disposal is when we drive past a chapel and see the broken-up pulpit and pews being piled into a skip or the archives being heaped onto a bonfire.

In a perfect world we would have a comprehensive record of every place of worship, compiled long before closures started in earnest. During 2014-18, to mark the centenary of the First World War, many communities researched the lives of the people commemorated by village war memorials. Could we persuade the historians in every community to do the same for the places of worship in their midst?

How about a Wikipedia page for every place of worship? Not only would future historians benefit, it is also likely that if the good folk of every community were to record their buildings, contents, archives, memorials and so on, they would begin to engage intellectually and emotionally with these places of worship and be more willing to intervene to save them if disposal were to be proposed. Otherwise they are invisible and do not even have a digital footprint.

Valuing the role of the building

We must also encourage a dialogue between the worshipping community and those members of the wider community who are not religious but who value the role of the building and the institution. Too often there is no dialogue at all, but my experience shows that it is not very difficult to get people to engage, with a little effort.

>>

"Enjoyment leads to a desire to understand heritage better."

Go thy Way

>>

For example, a church I know in Wiltshire built the necessary financial support to undertake vital repairs and re-ordering by opening the church for quiz nights, film shows, parties and concerts. They made the effort to reach out to the community and they did not put up barriers to access, saying in effect that all are welcome, not just people who subscribe to our beliefs. Congregations wedded to the idea that the church or chapel is for no other purpose than the worship of God and who lock the doors for all but an hour or so on a Sunday are the ones most likely to close.

It is vital that all who are in charge of churches and chapels in Wales embrace community use and recognise that it can also be a form of mission (although that is not the primary purpose of opening the doors and nothing will deter visitors more than the thought that if they enter a place of worship, somebody will try to 'convert' them).

Faith tourism

That brings me to faith tourism. This is a field in which the National Churches Trust and the Churches Conservation Trust have made a considerable investment, and we will watch with interest to see whether projects such as Experiencing Sacred Wales help to produce an income stream. The project managers have been working with the travel trade to create bookable tours, offering people the chance to visit faith buildings with a knowledgeable tour guide, travelling by bike, on foot, on horseback and by kayak. I am hopeful that a more professional and co-ordinated approach to faith tourism and pilgrimage, also being pioneered by the British Pilgrimage Trust, will yield positive results.

We should not assume, however, that faith tourism is the saviour for all our religious buildings. Another way forward would be a project similar to the National Churches Trust's 'House of Good' research report to measure the social and economic benefits of faith tourism and how effective this might be in securing the future of our faith buildings. We all say that faith tourism has enormous potential (it is worth £14 billion globally) but we need to know more about what works and whether the effort involved delivers the right results.

These are just some ideas for mitigating the accelerating rate of church and chapel closure and for protecting that precious legacy of buildings that form the quietly beating spiritual heart of every community. The alternative is to do nothing and see that legacy squandered in a generation.

Closure of places of worship also means that we lose a focus of community life, the place that serves for rites of passage – baptism, marriage, funerals and memorial services – and for national commemorations – Armistice, VE Day, Remembrance Day, not to mention festivals that may have pagan as well as Christian roots – Christmas and Easter, All Souls, Plough Sunday and Harvest Festival. We say goodbye to bells, flower festivals, choirs and musical recitals, a meeting space and a social place which guarantees some friendly company once a week.

Artistic, historical and architectural collections

Once a place of worship is sold, we no longer have access to the artistic, historical and architectural features of the building, nor to the social history inherent in the memorials, nor to the churchyard with its inscribed headstones and wildlife. We will no longer be able to discover and study the best collections of woodwork, sculpture, and stained glass to survive in Wales outside a museum.

The challenge now is to make sure that closure does not become the new post-Covid-19 normal, and I for one am determined to spend what remains of my life trying to ensure that it doesn't.

People like me who devote their lives to working in the heritage sector are motivated by the idea that there is a virtuous circle of conservation, which says that an initial connection with heritage arises when people enjoy visiting a historic place.

Enjoyment leads to a desire to understand the heritage better. Understanding leads people to value their heritage and this creates the possibility that they might be persuaded to take a role in caring for it. For the sake of the future of the UK's 39,000 places of worship, let us take this message forward and proclaim it whenever we hear the words 'church and chapel faces closure'.

Christopher Catling

Christopher Catling is Chair of The Welsh Places of Worship Forum and Secretary of The Royal Commission on the Ancient and Historical Monuments of Wales.

www.rcahmw.gov.uk
www.visitchurches.org.uk

Top: In 2020, BBC journalist and newsreader Huw Edwards, Vice President of the National Churches Trust, stood in the pulpit of Tabernacl Treforys (Morriston Tabernacle) to launch a campaign to raise funds to turn the chapel crypt into a café and community resource. Why, he asked, is so much public money spent on conserving ruined castles and abbeys, but not on such magnificent buildings as Morriston Tabernacle?

Middle: Listing is not always a protection against sale and disposal. The Grade II* listed church of St Mary, Llanfihangel-y-pennant, Gwynedd, has been sold and converted to holiday accommodation. Sensitive conversion has preserved such important features as the altar and the 15th-century timber roof, carved with grotesques and painted with red and white roses, but the character of the building has fundamentally change with public access lost.

Bottom: Welsh places of worship can look insignificant from the outside, but many of them contain furnishings, stained glass and memorials of real merit that are lost when the building is sold for development. Fortunately, Peniel Independent Chapel is now listed at Grade II as a well preserved example of an early nineteenth century rural chapel.

All © Christopher Catling

THE FUTURE OF THE UK's CHURCH BUILDINGS

65

THE UNITED KINGDOM

Scotland's *churches:* from surfeit to shortage?

Stuart Beattie
Director of Scotland's Churches Trust

> *"Scotland, for good historical reasons, had too many churches. It now risks having too few."*

Scotland's Churches Trust aims to advance the preservation, promotion and understanding of Scotland's churches and places of worship of all denominations. The challenges facing Scotland's places of worship in the post Covid world are similar to those being faced in the rest of the United Kingdom. Yet Scotland's religious history and its geography pose some unique challenges.

We were pleased to be asked our view as to the future of church buildings and as a member organisation we canvassed opinions and below share a small number of these.

Kenneth McLean a heritage professional, and a Church of Scotland Session Clerk, made the clear point that "a perfect way to 'save' churches is their continued use by healthy worshipping communities".

Ann Urwin, Session Clerk for the parish of Kilchrenan and Dalavich in Argyll, and typical of Scotland's rural churches, wanted to stress that the fellowship that is engendered at services makes churches very special places for local people. As she put it, they are "havens of peace and tranquility and at the same time a source of inspiration" and that would, of course, be lost should churches have to close.

David D Scot, a former Minister at Prestonkirk, East Linton, urged greater community use. He drew our attention to the way "some communities have been imaginative in buying church buildings and enhancing them for community use – worship, concerts, educational, conference and social space."

These include Kirkcaldy Old Kirk, which is now run by the local community and which Rosemary Potter from the Old Kirk Trust told us "has survived plague, fire and wars, and …will adapt to meet the new situation as it has in each generation through its thousand years of Christian worship and community service in the town."

A case for greater support by Government

Funding to keep places of worship open and in good repair remains a major challenge in Scotland, and Tom Ogilvie, a member of Christ Church in Falkirk, made a very pertinent point that "given that a substantial part of the desire to protect our heritage comes from the local community, it seems vital that they should assist with the financial resources required to maintain the buildings. The support of the community at large is currently generously provided by charitable trusts but there is a case for greater support by Government, whether at local or national levels."

I am appreciative of the time taken by members of Scotland's Churches Trust to share their views with us. The contribution of R D Kernohan, who has served as Church of Scotland elder in Glasgow's East End and at Cramond, Edinburgh, provided both a short history of Scotland's churches, useful for those who may be unfamiliar with it, and some possible solutions to the current impasse, directed primarily to the Church of Scotland, but more widely applicable. I reproduce a lightly edited version of his contribution below and hope that it stimulates thinking as to how best to sustain Scotland's places of worship.

"Scotland, for good historical reasons, had too many churches. It now risks having too few. It may also fail to ensure that they are in the best places for effective evangelism or to include all those of most historic or artistic importance. Such national landmarks as Glasgow Cathedral and St Giles' in Edinburgh may be safe but there is much more to our inheritance.

Duplication and triplication of buildings

"The patterns and the problems of Scotland's heritage of church buildings are very different from England's. Many of them still stem from the past divisions and subsequent reunions of Scottish Presbyterianism, which led to the duplication and often triplication of provision for buildings in the original parish system, and what now seems lavish over-provision in the Victorian age of urban expansion, some of it of an artistic merit only recently rediscovered.

>>

Scotland's *churches:* from surfeit to shortage?

\>\>

"The situation was compounded by the prosperous enthusiasm of the Episcopalians to create a national network of churches – from tiny chapels to the grandeur of St Mary's Cathedral in Edinburgh's West End. There were more haphazard achievements of other denominations, such as the once-great Baptist temple of the Coats Memorial in Paisley, now an "events venue", though a sale to modern Baptists has saved St George's West and its Victorian-Venetian campanile in Edinburgh.

"Roman Catholics were less ambitious and prolific in church architecture, except for a spell in the mid-twentieth century, and their problems with surplus buildings probably count for less than a shortage of priests to serve them.

"As a result, Scotland's Churches, and especially the Kirk, have struggled over the past century to adjust an over-supply of buildings to a gradually decreasing demand and at the same time to provide churches in newly created or vastly changed areas of housing development. In the inter-war and post-war periods they succeeded fairly well. More recently it has perhaps been evident that their strength, and perhaps their confidence, are unequal to their task. Developments which would once have merited new buildings are left unchurched, although existing parishes struggle to serve them.

An anti-building complex

"In this situation it may not be surprising that there are signs in the Church, more evident among ministers than congregations, of an anti-building complex. Ministers, who are local chief executives as well as chief pastors and teaching elders, often growl at the time, effort, and money that goes to maintaining venerable buildings and patching up more modern ones. Church leaders have insisted that the church is not a curator of historic buildings.

"The Church is never its buildings and must never worship them, but most of its people and its congregations feel the need for a hub that becomes a holy place. We need the spiritual dimension that comes from gathering to share our faith and sometimes to sustain our faith. We need a base for our activities and good works and where we can invite others to join in them. And though we live in the present and for the future we are the better for being reminded of those who passed before us and whom we sometimes feel around us.

"Unfortunately there is a real risk now in Scotland that reduction in the number of ministers and churches will create parishes so large that they are increasingly divorced from local communities, whether in scattered rural settings or the 'urban villages' still often discernible in big cities. But risks are more obvious than answers and even mitigations can be difficult.

A spiritual, historic and artistic inheritance

"Two changes of emphasis in current thinking would help. One is to separate as far as possible decisions on the number of church buildings and "worship stations" from the question of how many full-time ministers can be recruited and afforded. That depends on a readiness in all denominations to rediscover in a contemporary form (involving, for example, the Kirk's elders) the impetus that Methodism once gained from its local preachers.

"Another is for there to be more devolution to local congregations of decisions about buildings, qualified by a stronger national and denominational acceptance that a curacy of spiritual, historic, and artistic inheritance should be a duty and delight as well as a burden. There is room in the Church for gathered congregations as well as parish ones, and there is also a need for churches to relate consciously to the needs and daily life of a community, in most cases a territorial one.

"Members of the Church should not feel guilty when they 'take pleasure in her stones and favour the dust thereof' and the humblest and most disposable of church properties have hallowed human associations and are remembered in the listed buildings of Heaven. Nor should they feel guilty when they ensure that they allow for flexible forms of worship and provide a focus for the social and cultural life of all ages in the communities they serve."

Stuart Beattie

In 2010 Stuart Beattie was invited to become Director of the Scottish Churches Architectural Heritage Trust, and following the merger with Scotland's Churches Scheme became Director of Scotland's Churches Trust, developing the Trust to make it a sector leader and to grow it so that its aim of offering sustainability to Scotland's working churches can be achieved.

www.scotlandschurchestrust.org.uk

Top: Under stormy skies, Lochailort Church stands alone on remote moorland in the west Highlands of Scotland
© Joe Dunckley / Alamy Stock Photo
Bottom: St Machar Cathedral, Aberdeen © LDN Architects

THE FUTURE OF THE UK's CHURCH BUILDINGS

THE UNITED KINGDOM

England's rural churches *through* all ages

Dr Julian Litten FSA
Architectural historian

"A home from home, a place of worship, of mission, of companionship, of comfort, of rest, of sorrow, of rapture and of joy. This is what a church building should be."

The recent pandemic saw – and, in some places, continues to see – alterations in access to our churches. In June this year I returned to Thaxted, an exceptionally beautiful small town where it was my privilege to live and worship between 1983 and 1996. The parish church there is of cathedral proportions and, sitting high on a hill, dominates the town. However, as with all churches, its beauty lies within.

This elegant East Anglian building with its closely-set Perpendicular nave windows is full of space and light – the best comparison in the county where I now live – Norfolk – being the church of St Peter, Walpole St Peter. The vista from the west door at Thaxted to the high altar at the east end is a vision of loveliness, harmony and subtle colour. In short, it is probably one of the finest church interiors I know. I more than like it; I love it.

A home from home, a place of worship, of mission, of companionship, of comfort, of rest, of sorrow, of rapture and of joy. This is what a church building should be. Thaxted church means all of this to me, and then to be denied access because of a pandemic filled me with sadness. Not even during our darkest hours of the Great War and WWII was this building ever closed, and now it was shut owing to an unseen enemy, the invisible COVID Angel of Death.

And yet this did not apply only to Thaxted. Thousands of churches across the land were under the same restrictions. Yes, I'm mindful that we do not need church buildings to worship God as that can be done anywhere, in our hearts, our minds and our souls. But, as Christians, we are an Easter People and, as people, we need one another and, to be blunt, we need to worship together; and yet COVID has denied us that fellowship.

The jewel in the crown

Norfolk and Suffolk have the finest churches in England, taken all round, both counties being very little known except to the most dedicated of church-crawlers. It is my privilege to be closely connected with both, as Chairman of Norwich Cathedral Fabric Advisory Committee and the St Edmundsbury Cathedral Fabric Advisory Committee. Of the two dioceses, Norfolk has the most churches – 666 in all (curiously, the Number of the Beast) – of which more than 600 are rural, each and every one of them the jewel in the crown of the villages and hamlets in which they stand.

All of these churches have served us well over the centuries. They are places where we come to give thanks, to exercise the milestones of our own lives – baptism, marriage and, finally, death – where we receive strength through the Blessed Sacrament and where we can unite in fellowship to experience a foretaste of the Kingdom of Heaven; they are our pathway to the Eternal City. It is in that unity of fellowship where church buildings serve us best. Furthermore, they could and should become places of formal gathering, for the churched and the unchurched, the Christian and the non-believer.

Prayers of the poor

There were days when it was my privilege to sit in Thaxted church on my own, time which allowed me to reflect on its importance to the town, how it had withstood and held fast during the Black Death, the Peasants' Revolt, the Reformation, the Civil War and the two World Wars. In the chancel are the ledger-stones of the town's wealthier inhabitants of the 17th and 18th centuries, but of greater importance to me was that the walls of the entire building had been impregnated over the centuries with the prayers of the poor, those who are 'dearer to God'.

> *"To make our churches the multi-purpose public spaces they can be in a hurting world that has never needed them more."*

England's rural churches through all ages

>>

To some extent it does not matter that church-going is in decline for our responsibility is to keep the flame alive. The Holy Spirit knows when to stir the heart and whilst few of us will live to see the revival, that revival will certainly come. But, in the meantime, how can we make use of our churches, apart from that of worship?

If used sensitively they could provide those valuable services which villages have lost, in the same way that some pubs (provided that there is still a pub) support a district post office and a local surgery. Church buildings are eminently flexible, and there is no reason why they cannot be a place of public meeting, a concert hall, a place for sales of work and Fairtrade merchandise, for exhibitions, to host craft and conservation workshops and much more. In the more rural areas, why not make it the drop off/pick up point for items purchased on line? Far better than making a special journey to town.

A home from home

For many years I've wondered why a church building cannot be a place to support community events and - dare one say it – even being used as a Wedding Venue? Why do baptism parties, wedding receptions and funeral wakes have to be held elsewhere than in the very church in which the event has taken place? In days past the nave was used for so many communal activities, a real example of living Christian Socialism. Put bluntly, church buildings should be as flexible as ourselves. And how about using our rural churches as a home-from-home for the lonely, where they can socialise and have a cup of coffee and cake and a good old natter?

The mid-20th century church historian Lawrence Jones, summed up English churches well when he said that "If, however, these churches are to attain their full and lasting beauty, that beauty will not only exist in the craftsmanship, but more and more it will be in the lives of those who use the churches, growing more and more like the life of Him who is our one and only pattern, Our Blessed Saviour Jesus Christ." And using such buildings for purposes additional to worship would, surely, create a cohesive and caring local community.

Julian Litten FSA

Dr Julian Litten is an architectural historian and is chairman of the Norwich Cathedral Fabric Advisory Committee and of the St Edmundsbury Cathedral Fabric Advisory Committee as well as being a member of the Westminster Abbey Fabric Commission and the Ely Cathedral Fabric Advisory Committee.

Top: The church of St John the Baptist, St Mary and St Lawrence, Thaxted © Peter Etteridge/Alamy Stock Photo
Bottom: St Lawrence church, Bardney, Lincolnshire © ExploreChurces

THE UNITED KINGDOM

An iconic *part of the historic environment of* Northern Ireland

Iain Greenway
Director of Historic Environment
in the Department for Communities
(Northern Ireland)

"Churches are the buildings which have been the focus of communities over many years and they reflect that investment of time and hard cash."

Northern Ireland has a wide and varied legacy of church buildings left to it by past generations. Indeed, the current generation has provided some very fine additions to this group. These buildings are found right across the region, in every village and town, and also in some apparently very isolated locations.

Everywhere they are an expression of community, of a history of worship, of values beyond the material word and, in a place where divisions can sometimes run deep, they are a reminder of the common Christian values that have formed our communities. It is an important legacy to be valued and cherished.

Compared to other parts of the UK, this group is very different. It has been formed by the particular history of this place. For example, there are only two medieval churches in Northern Ireland that are roofed and still used for worship, and two heavily altered cathedrals.

Most of our medieval churches are ruins, often in the graveyard beside the current building. The reason for this is largely a result of historical events. Many buildings were destroyed or significantly damaged in the great upheaval of the Ulster Plantation in the early Seventeenth century. Often they were patched up and remained in use until the early nineteenth century.

Then, significant money was invested by the Government in the Church of Ireland following the Act of Union of 1801, and this resulted in 20 to 30 years of new church building. The 'tower and hall' Church of Ireland church is common throughout the island as a result – a rectangular hall of classical proportion, often with battlements and some gothic windows with a tall tower at the entrance. Catholics and Nonconformists – mainly Presbyterian in Northern Ireland- were barred by the Penal Laws enacted in the late seventeenth century by the Irish Parliament from erecting spires on their places of worship.

As a result, these denominations erected very similar buildings. Often a simple hall, these developed into T shaped buildings as congregations grew in size. The focus of the building tended to be on the long wall of the hall. For Catholics this was focused upon the altar and for Presbyterians the focus was the pulpit.

Significant numbers of new churches were built

In the second half of the Nineteenth century significant numbers of new churches were built particularly in the booming town of Belfast which was rapidly expanding. These buildings followed the architectural styles common across the UK at the time: an increasing sophistication of gothic forms; Ruskinian influenced polychromatic buildings; and Italianate and classical revival buildings.

Emigration to America resulted in significant remittances to the Catholic authorities and the building of expensive and detailed churches and cathedrals. In some places the Presbyterians and Methodists rose to the challenge and upgraded and enhanced the facades of plainer buildings – a competition to deliver architectural quality that benefited the whole community.

In the Twentieth century, church building continued often in the new suburbs and there are good examples from the period, many listed by my Department as buildings of special architectural and historic interest. There was also change brought about as denominations responded to new conditions – Vatican 2 in the Roman Catholic Church leading to significant internal alteration in many buildings from the late 1960's; and alterations in many Presbyterian and Methodist churches in recent years to provide community facilities and more flexible liturgical spaces.

This legacy provides a touchstone to our history. Churches are the buildings which have been the focus of communities over many years and they reflect that investment of time and hard cash. In many places they are the single conscious piece of architecture, built by commissioned architects or bearing the marks of special treatment over many generations.

An important cultural symbol

In a time when fewer people may use them than in previous generations, they remain an important cultural symbol to the wider community. It is a truism to point out that, as with many historic places, people may not even have ever visited them, they may even associate with a different denomination or none

>>

THE FUTURE OF THE UK's CHURCH BUILDINGS

> *"People will always have a deep affinity with their place and its principal community spaces. If these buildings continue to be used for the purpose intended, that helps to reinforce a continuity with the past that most people will continue to value."*

An iconic part of the historic environment of Northern Ireland

\>\>

at all, but their continued presence provides an important part of their identity. They symbolise the place they are from and how they understand their community.

Moving forward, that is unlikely to change: people will always have a deep affinity with their place and its principal community spaces. If these buildings continue to be used for the purpose intended, that helps to reinforce a continuity with the past that most people will continue to value.

But numbers attending regular church services have been falling in Northern Ireland over the last twenty years. While not yet reduced to the levels seen in other parts of the UK, there is a need to be creative about use and utilisation, if the buildings are to be sustained as churches into the future. I see much evidence of such creativity, including the increasing use of the buildings for secular events such as concerts, talks and tours to bring in the wider community.

The conversion of a Presbyterian church on the Ards peninsula to an arts centre that still holds regular worship on a Sunday is one extreme example. The work of the National Churches Trust is very important in this regard. The Places of Worship Forum which we have supported the Trust to hold over recent years has allowed a sharing of information between congregations and denominations that was not there before and has also allowed experience from 'across the water' to be understood.

Our rich legacy of historic buildings

In Historic Environment Division we have been upon a wider journey over recent years. This has been to highlight the benefit of the whole historic environment to Northern Ireland's communities and its decision makers. We have partnered with stakeholders across the heritage sector to produce a document and website – Heritage Delivers (www.NIheritagedelivers.org) that sets out how our rich legacy of historic buildings, monuments, landscapes and marine features contributes to our society, economy, and environment.

We are working closely with partners across the sector and across government to realise the full potential of these assets. Our church buildings, such an iconic part of our historic environment, are key to this and we were delighted to be able to partner with the National Churches Trust last year to provide Covid-19 recovery funding aimed at ensuring that these important buildings can be maintained for the future and utilised for the benefit of all.

Moving forward, many challenges will remain; but I am sure that with effort, partnership and good will, these vital buildings will continue to enjoy a bright future.

Iain Greenway

Iain Greenway is Director of Historic Environment in the Department for Communities (Northern Ireland), overseeing the delivery of work to help communities to enjoy and realise the value of the historic environment.

www.communities-ni.gov.uk/landing-pages/historic-environment

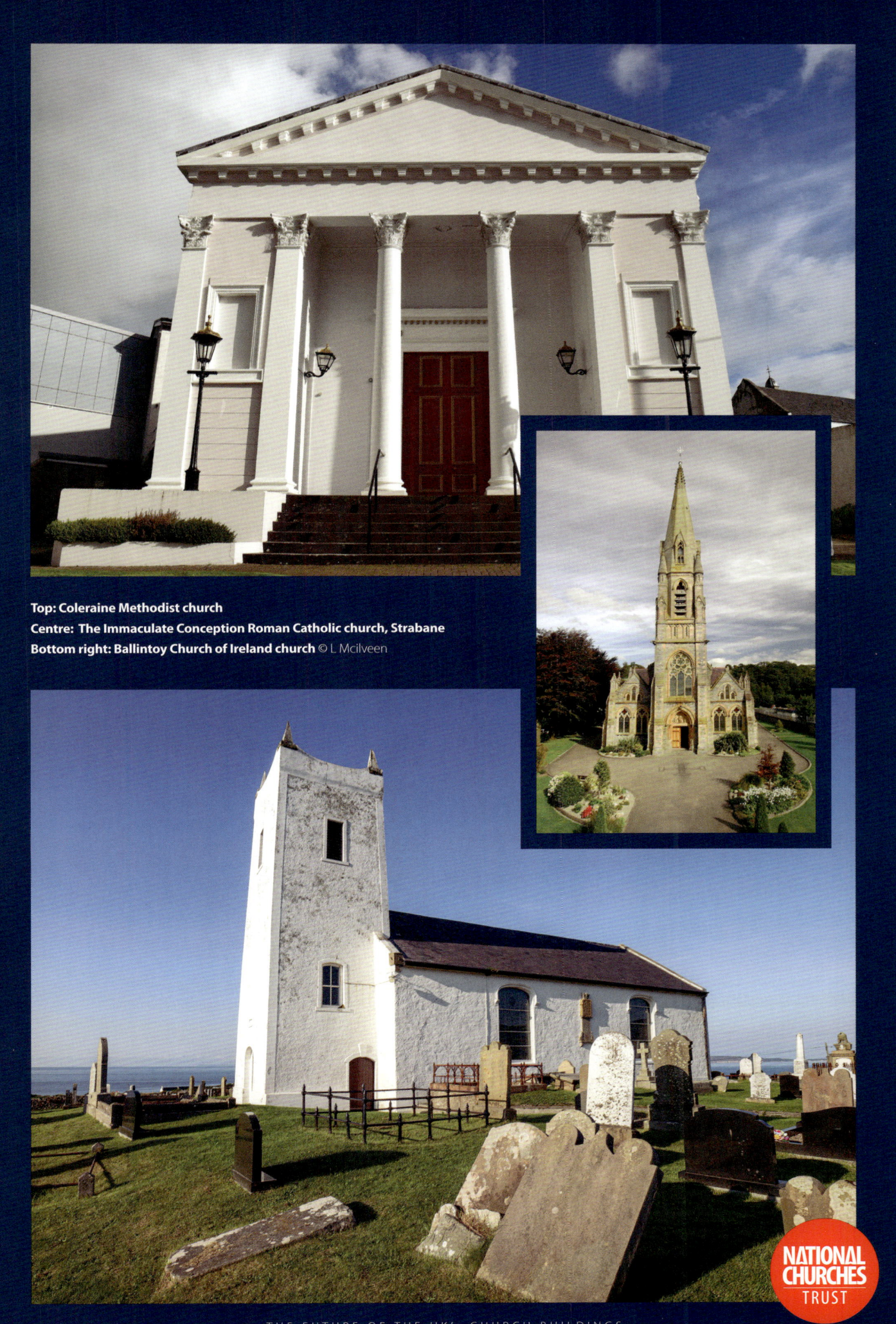

Top: Coleraine Methodist church
Centre: The Immaculate Conception Roman Catholic church, Strabane
Bottom right: Ballintoy Church of Ireland church © L Mcilveen

THE FUTURE OF THE UK's CHURCH BUILDINGS

Factfile

1. Number of church buildings in the UK

There were around 39,800 church buildings in the UK open to the public and being used for worship in 2020, according to research carried out for the National Churches Trust by the Brierley Consultancy.

The number of church buildings is substantially higher than other key public buildings in the UK. There are currently around 39,130 pubs (ONS 2019), 11,500 post office branches (Post Office 2020), 9,500 bank or building society branches (2020 House of Commons library) and 3,600 public libraries (The Reading Agency 2019-20).

Estimated number of church buildings in the UK by denomination.

Anglican	16,600
Methodist	4,400
Presbyterian	4,100
Roman Catholic	3,700
Independent	4,900
Baptist	3,100
Smaller denominations	1,400
Pentecostal	1,600
Orthodox	200

The number of Christian congregations in the UK is around 45,000. This figure is higher than the number of church buildings as some are used by more than one congregation or worship takes place in a school or community hall.

2. The social and economic value of the UK's church buildings

From foodbanks to credit unions, churches across the UK provide a growing list of essential services for people in urgent need.

In 2020, for the very first time, the National Churches Trust's The House of Good report quantified the economic and social value of all church buildings in the UK. Not just the bricks and mortar but the welfare and wellbeing they create.

The House of Good report showed that the total economic and social value that church buildings generate in the UK is at least £12.4 billion per year which averages around £300,000 per church. That is roughly equal to the total NHS spending on mental health in England in 2018. For every £10 invested there is a return of at least £37.40.

The HM Treasury Green Book published supplementary guidance in July 2021. This has had the effect of increasing the yearly social value of UK churches and the activities taking place in them to around £55.7 billion.

That is roughly twice as much as the total spend on adult social care by local authorities.

THE HOUSE OF GOOD

3. Number of listed church buildings

England has 14,500 listed places of worship (4,000 Grade I, 4,500 Grade II* and 6,000 Grade II). 45% of all Grade I listed buildings are places of worship.

There are 3,000 listed places of worship in Wales, 1,689 in Scotland and 920 in Northern Ireland.

4. Funding of church buildings

To remain open and sustainable, church buildings need to be in good repair, well maintained and with a range of community facilities to help serve the needs of local people.

Many people think that church authorities or government pay for the upkeep of the UK's church buildings. But it is up to parishes and congregations to raise the money to fix a leaking roof or install toilets. In many cases it is impossible for them to raise the money themselves.

That is why in recent years the UK's mixed economy of local funding, national philanthropy from trusts and foundations and Government and heritage body grants has been essential to keep church buildings open and in good repair and to safeguard their future.

Demand for funds to carry out urgent repairs and provide community facilities far exceeds supply. In 2020, the National Churches Trust had to turn away three out of every four applications such was the scale of funding requests.

The COVID-19 pandemic and lockdowns have exacerbated the situation, with churches closed for long periods of time and unable to raise income from their many activities, including normal collections.

The support provided by the Cultural Recovery Fund has proved a life saver to many parish churches and other places of worship.

Most recently in October 2021, it provided funding of £12 million to help fund the repair of churches, chapels and cathedrals in England.

The fact remains that there is a lack of long term funding from Government and heritage bodies for urgent repairs and the maintenance of church buildings. This is of of great concern to those tasked with managing and running the UK's church buildings.

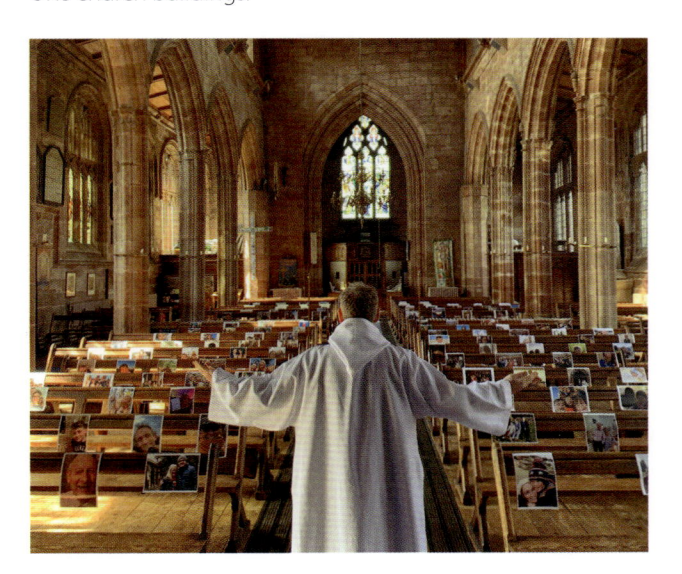

National funding schemes

Cultural Recovery Fund

The Government's Culture Recovery Fund has helped thousands of culture and heritage organisations, including local parish churches across the country, survive the COVID pandemic, the biggest crisis they've ever faced.

Listed Places of Worship Grant Scheme

The Listed Places of Worship Grant Scheme repays VAT incurred in making repairs to listed buildings mainly used for public worship throughout the UK.

National Heritage Lottery Fund

Since 2018, the National Heritage Lottery Fund no longer operates a separate Grants for Places of Worship scheme, which provided a dedicated funding stream for church buildings. Instead churches and other places of worship apply along with everyone else for the general open grant programmes. NHLF grants have tended to favour heritage education and community related projects rather than repairs.

Wales

The Community Facilities Programme is a capital grant scheme operated by the Welsh Government and which is open to places of worship. Grants can be used to improve community facilities which are useful to, and well used by, people in the community.

The Welsh Church Act Fund is administered by local authorities in Wales. Grants are available for the repair and restoration of historic religious and secular buildings, especially when in community use.

Scotland

Historic Environment Scotland (formerly Historic Scotland) can provide grants of between £10,000 - £500,000 to support conservation-standard repair projects across Scotland which secure the original fabric of historic buildings and ancient monuments using traditional materials and skills.

Local funding

Local Authorities very rarely contribute towards the costs incurred on the repairs or maintenance of church buildings as it is unclear whether they are legally allowed to do so.

THE FUTURE OF THE UK's CHURCH BUILDINGS

Join the debate

1. What do you think are the main purposes of church buildings?

☐ Places of worship   ☐ National heritage   ☐ Community hubs

OTHER (please add) ⬜

2. Are church buildings assets or burdens?

☐ Assets   ☐ Burdens

3. Who should be responsible for funding the repair and maintenance of church buildings (tick more than one)?

☐ Congregations   ☐ Denominations

☐ Central Government and Devolved Administrations

☐ Heritage Bodies such as the NHLF

☐ Local Councils   ☐ Local Businesses

☐ Charitable Trusts and Foundations

OTHER (please add) ⬜

4. Have digital services reduced the need for church buildings?

☐ Yes   ☐ No   ☐ Don't know

5. Should congregations share church buildings so that, perhaps, fewer buildings are needed overall?

☐ Yes   ☐ No   ☐ Don't know

6. If a church is threatened with closure, should local people be able to take ownership of the building so it can be used as:

☐ a community asset

☐ a place of worship

OTHER (please add) ⬜

NATIONAL CHURCHES TRUST

Now that you've read what other people have to say about church buildings, we'd like to hear what you think.

Below are six questions we'd like you to answer.

There is also space for additional comments.

You can complete this online at:
www.nationalchurchestrust.org/futureofchurches

Your comments

Please use this space to make any other comments or to share your ideas with us.

Your name (optional)

Your email (optional)

Are you a regular churchgoer? ☐ Yes ☐ No

Do you visit churches as a tourist? ☐ Yes ☐ No

Do you use a church for community purposes? ☐ Yes ☐ No

Are you a Friend of the National Churches Trust? ☐ Yes ☐ No

Please fill in this form and return to us at:

**Future of Churches,
National Churches Trust,
7 Tufton Street,
London SW1P 3QB**

We take your privacy seriously and treat all the personal data you give us with great care. We will not sell or swap your details with any other organisation, ever, and will keep your details private and secure. Our Privacy Policy at www.nationalchurchestrust.org/privacypolicy explains how we collect, store and use the personal data you give to us.

Your name and/or email will only be used to contact you about this survey.

Sending you information about our work

We would like to send you our monthly e-newsletter and occasional invitations to events and updates to our work. You can opt out at any time.

☐ YES, please keep me informed about your work by email

About the National Churches Trust

Our vision and mission

Our vision is that church buildings across the UK are well maintained, open to everyone, sustainable and valued.

Our mission is to help keep the UK's wonderful collection of church buildings well maintained, valued and used.

The United Kingdom has some of the most historic and beautiful religious buildings to be found anywhere in the world. At the centre of local communities, churches, chapels and meeting houses provide a home for countless activities such as playgroups, drop-in-centres and musical events, as well as serving their core purpose as places of worship.

Please support our work

In 2020, we provided £1.7 million of grants to churches and chapels for urgent repairs, essential maintenance and the installation of community facilities. It is thanks to our Friends and supporters that we are able to help the UK's churches, chapels and meeting houses.

Become a Friend

As a Friend of the National Churches Trust, you'll help us protect even more church buildings. Choose from individual, joint or lifetime membership.

nationalchurchestrust.org/membership

Stay connected

Sign up for our e-newsletter and find us on social media to see more about how we're saving the UK's church buildings.

nationalchurchestrust.org/enews

Make a donation

A one-off or monthly gift will fund community facilities and essential maintenance – and ensure more church buildings remain at the heart of their local communities.

nationalchurchestrust.org/donate

All the essays remain the intellectual property of the authors and are protected by international copyright law.

The opinions expressed do not necessarily reflect those of The National Churches Trust but remain solely those of the authors.

Images are the intellectual property of the relevant photographers unless otherwise stated We have attempted to trace the copyright of the photographers but have not been able to do so in all cases. No attribution does not imply that the work is the copyright of the National Churches Trust